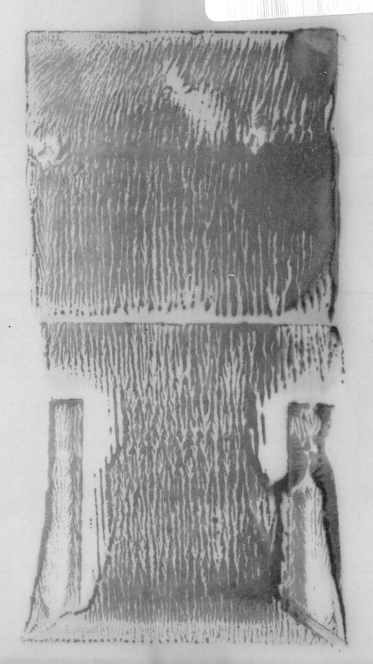

MORAL RULES
AND
PARTICULAR
CIRCUMSTANCES

CENTRAL ISSUES IN PHILOSOPHY SERIES

BARUCH A. BRODY
series editor

edited by

BARUCH A. BRODY
Massachusetts Institute of Technology

MORAL RULES

AND

PARTICULAR

CIRCUMSTANCES

Prentice-Hall, Inc., Englewood Cliffs, New Jersey

Library of Congress Catalog Card Number: 75–106507

Printed in the United States of America

C 13–600874–7
P 13–600866–6

Current Printing (last digit):

10   9   8   7   6   5   4   3   2   1

PRENTICE-HALL INTERNATIONAL, INC., London
PRENTICE-HALL OF AUSTRALIA, PTY. LTD., Sydney
PRENTICE-HALL OF CANADA, LTD., Toronto
PRENTICE-HALL OF INDIA PRIVATE LIMITED, New Delhi
PRENTICE-HALL OF JAPAN, INC., Tokyo

Foreword

~~~~~~

The Central Issues in Philosophy series is based upon the conviction that the best way to teach philosophy to introductory students
is to experience or to *do* philosophy with them. The basic unit of
philosophical investigation is the particular problem, and not the
area or the historical figure. Therefore, this series consists of sets of
readings organised around well-defined, manageable problems. All
other things being equal, problems that are of interest and relevance
to the student have been chosen.

Each volume contains an introduction that clearly defines the
problem and sets out the alternative positions that have been taken.
The selections are chosen and arranged in such a way as to take the
student through the dialectic of the problem; each reading, besides
presenting a particular point of view, criticizes the points of view
set out earlier.

Although no attempt has been made to introduce the student in a
systematic way to the history of philosophy, classical selections
relevant to the development of the problem have been included. As
a side benefit, the student will therefore come to see the continuity,
as well as the breaks, between classical and contemporary thought.
But in no case has a selection been included merely for its historical
significance; clarity of expression and systematic significance are the
main criteria for selection.

<div align="right">Baruch A. Brody</div>

Contents

Introduction

People offer many types of arguments to defend their moral views about what is right and what is wrong in particular cases. This volume is concerned with the relative significance of two of these types of arguments, and with the moral problems that arise when these arguments lead to conflicting conclusions.

When called upon to defend one's view that an action is right or wrong, one very often appeals to a moral rule. Thus, the view that it is wrong for Jones to keep money that belongs to someone else might be defended by saying that this would be stealing and it is wrong to steal. The moral rule appealed to is the rule against stealing. In other cases, however, one defends one's view of an action as right or wrong by pointing to the good or bad consequences of the action in question. Thus, one might defend the view that it is wrong for Jones, who can easily help the man in need, to refuse him help, on the grounds that this refusal would lead to a great deal of suffering and unhappiness.

A most difficult moral problem arises when these two types of moral arguments lead to conflicting conclusions. The following cases, some taken from the philosophical literature and others from more popular writings, are good examples of this type of problem.

1. Someone has loaned you his hunting gun, and you have promised to return it when he asks for it. He comes to you one day and asks for it; you see from his actions that he intends to use it to hurt or kill someone. Should you return it to him, or should you break

1

your promise by lying and saying that you don't have it at the moment? The moral rules against lying and breaking one's promises seem to imply that the gun should be returned, and that one should not lie about where it is. On the other hand, it seems that the consequences would be better if you did lie to him and did not keep your promise to return the gun.

2. An old friend of yours who is dying tells you where he has hidden some money, and makes you promise to give it to his favorite charity. He dies and you find the money. But you know that his charity has plenty of money, while there is a different charity with a far greater need. The moral rules about keeping promises, being true to one's friends, and a man's having the right to do what he wants with his money all seem to imply that you should give the money to his charity. However, it might seem that better consequences would result if you broke these rules and gave the money to the charity that had the greater need.

3. You are the chief of police in a small town in which a hideous murder has been committed, and you have no evidence as to who committed the crime. A lynch mob in the street will soon murder many innocent people, and the only way to stop these additional murders is to frame someone. You have in jail an old drunken hobo who is dying. Should you frame him to save the many lives that would otherwise be lost? The moral rules against harming the innocent, perverting justice, and so on, all seem to imply that he should not be framed. On the other hand, better consequences would probably come about if you did frame the old man.

4. The boat you were on sank, and you are with a group of survivors on a lifeboat that is sinking because there are too many people on it. Unless several people are pushed off, you will all die. Someone has proposed a lottery as a fair method of choosing the victims. Although the moral rule against murder seems to imply that you should not hold such a lottery, it seems that better consequences (the survival of more people) would come about if you did hold the lottery and push off the losers.

5. You are the citizen of a society which, although normally quite just and fair, has recently adopted a law which will bring much suffering to one minority group. The law requires you to do certain actions which will produce these undesirable consequences. The moral rules about obedience to the laws seem to imply that you should do these actions, but it seems that better consequences would ensue if you refused to obey that law.

In some of the above cases, it seems clear that one ought to follow the moral rule; others seem to require the action that will lead to the best consequences. In some, it is not certain what one ought to do. A consideration of these cases seems to lead to the following basic issue in moral philosophy: under what conditions, if any, should obedience to a moral rule take precedence over an action that will lead to the best consequences, and under what conditions, if any, should doing what will lead to the best consequences take precedence over obedience to a moral rule?

There is another way of looking at this problem. In each of the above cases, the proponent of breaking the moral rule is, in effect, claiming that the mere fact that breaking the rule will lead to better consequences, justifies making an exception to it, while his opponent denies this. So a consideration of these cases also leads to another basic issue in moral philosophy: under what conditions, if any, should one make exceptions to moral rules?

Classical moral philosophers can be divided into two groups on these issues. The deontological moralists have claimed that an action is right only if it is in accord with the correct moral rules, and wrong only if it violates these rules. According to the deontological position, one should follow the moral rules in all cases, and disregard the fact that such action may lead to bad consequences. This position seems to allow for no exceptions to moral rules. The teleological moralists, on the other hand, have claimed that an action is right only if it leads to the best possible consequences, and wrong otherwise. According to this position, one should always do what leads to the best consequences, disregarding the fact that this may mean violating many moral rules. This position is quite prepared to allow for exceptions to moral rules.

There are a great many different types of deontological and teleological moral systems. This volume begins with the Kantian version of the deontological position and the Sidgwickian version of the teleological position. They have been chosen primarily because of their intrinsic interest, but also because they present the deontological and teleological positions in an unadulterated fashion. The reader should keep in mind that there are many other versions of these two positions, and he will have to decide for himself whether objections that are raised are objections to the deontological or teleological moralities in general, or merely to the Kantian or Sidgwickian versions of these moralities.

There are two problems that any deontological system of morality must face: (a) According to the deontological position, an action is right if and only if it is in accord with the correct moral rules, and wrong if and only if it violates them. But which of the many moral rules that might be proposed are the correct ones? (b) Can, and should, a deontological position be modified to allow for exceptions to its seemingly rigid moral rules? Kant addressed himself to both of these issues.

Kant seems to propose a universal test for deciding whether a moral rule upon which a person considers acting (a moral maxim) is a correct moral rule. According to this test, a moral maxim would be a correct moral rule if and only if one could will it as a universal law of action. The reader will have to decide for himself whether Kant was correct in supposing that this test could be used to draw the distinction between correct and incorrect moral rules.

In the second part of the selection from Kant, he considers the claim that there should be exceptions to moral rules, such as the rule about telling the truth, when these exceptions will produce beneficial consequences. Kant explains why he feels that such exceptions cannot be allowed in any true system of morality, and also argues that one is not doing wrong when one follows the rule, even if the consequences are very bad.

A third major problem faced by any deontological position is not dealt with by Kant. As Sidgwick points out, we often face moral problems because two different moral rules seem to have conflicting consequences. Consider the following example of such a moral problem: I have promised a friend that I will protect his family while he is away, but the only way that I can do that is by telling a lie that will prevent someone from harming them. One moral rule (about keeping promises) implies that I should protect his family by telling the lie, while another rule (about telling the truth) implies that I should not tell the lie. What is one supposed to do, according to the deontological morality, in these cases of conflicting rules? Doesn't this type of case render a deontological morality incoherent?

This problem of conflicting moral rules, together with the feeling that the deontological morality, despite Kant's arguments, is mistaken in not allowing for exceptions to moral rules, has led many philosophers, such as Sidgwick, to reject the deontological morality in favor of some version of a teleological moral system. The form of teleological morality that Sidgwick adopts is the position of *utilitarianism* (which he sometimes calls *universalistic hedonism*). According to this position, an action is right if and only if it will, in the given circumstances, produce the greatest amount of happiness for all those affected by the action.

It is easy to see how this position avoids the problems faced by deontological moral systems. If following a moral rule in a case leads to less happiness than would come about if the moral rule were broken, then the utilitarian position would endorse breaking the moral rule. The utilitarian position is therefore able to allow for the legitimate exceptions for which the deontological position cannot allow. Similarly, in cases of conflicting moral rules, the utilitarian tells you to follow that rule (if any) such that following it in this case would lead to the most happiness for those involved. The utilitarian position, unlike the deontological position, can tell you what to do when there are conflicting moral rules covering a single case.

It is easy to see why the utilitarian position avoids the difficulties of deontological morality. Utilitarian morality, by evaluating an action in terms of its consequences rather than in terms of moral rules, offers something more basic than moral rules to which we can appeal, and it is this basic standard that allows for exceptions and resolves problems of conflicting moral rules. But one must not suppose that the utilitarian moralist wants to do away with the standard moral rules. Sidgwick argues, quite convincingly, that many of our traditional moral rules (he calls them the *morality of common sense*) that tell us to do actions of type *x* and not of type *y* are based upon past realization that doing *x* and not doing *y* leads to the most happiness for those concerned. So, says Sidgwick, a utilitarian will usually follow most of the standard moral rules, those that are based on these considerations and not upon various prejudices, and will break them only when it is clear that doing so will lead to the most happiness. According to Sidgwick, utilitarianism is not as radical a position as it might seem at first glance.

Although utilitarianism has numerous merits, many philosophers have found serious flaws in it. To begin with, as Ross points out, utilitarianism recognizes the maximization of human happiness as our only essential moral obligation, with the happiness of any human being counting just as much as, but no more than, that of any other human being. How can utilitarianism then account for our special moral obligations to members of our family, friends, and fellow citizens? Second, as Harrison indicates, certain actions which seem to be our duty to perform do not produce human happiness. Consider, for example, one's duty to vote in an election for the candidate one thinks best. We all recognize that, barring some extraordinary accident, a single vote will not make any difference to the outcome of the election, so one can hardly claim a duty to vote because this will increase the sum total of human happiness. How is the utilitarian to explain this and other such moral obligations?

These two objections, while serious, do not really touch upon the major difficulty with Sidgwick's utilitarianism. The real problem is that the position seems to allow for too many exceptions to our moral rules. As Ross says, utilitarianism implies that a moral rule ought to be broken as soon as the total happiness to be produced by breaking the rule exceeds, even infinitesimally, the total happiness that would be produced by following it. This certainly seems counterintuitive, since, while we do think that rules should sometimes be broken in order to maximize human happiness, we demand that breaking the rule produce a significant increase in human happiness. For example, you should break a promise to save a life, but not simply because breaking it will make just one person a little bit happier.

We should not be surprised that the utilitarian position allows for too many exceptions. After all, as the cases considered at the beginning of this introduction suggested, when following moral rules will conflict with attainment of the most happiness, we should sometimes do what will produce the most happiness, and we should sometimes follow the rules. Therefore, if Kant's deontological morality is mistaken in claiming that we should always follow the moral rules, Sidgwick's teleological morality is equally mistaken in stating that we should always make an exception to the rule and do what will lead to the best consequences.

Is there any way of forming a theory of morality that avoids the extreme positions of Sidgwick and Kant? The search for such a theory has been one of the main concerns of twentieth-century ethics. Contemporary writers have been searching for a system that combines the deontologist's emphasis on rules with the teleologist's emphasis upon the consequences of actions. The two major positions that have been proposed are Ross's theory of *prima facie obligations* and *rule-utilitarianism,* the position advocated by (among others) Harrison.

Ross is trying to construct a deontological system that can deal with the problem of conflicting moral rules and allow for the correctness, on at least some occasions, of breaking a moral rule in order to maximize human happiness. He proposes modifying the deontological position so that: (a) the moral rules, rather than asserting that one ought to do *x* or ought not do *y*, merely assert that one has a *prima facie* obligation to do *x* or a *prima facie* obligation not to do *y*; and (b) one of the moral rules would be that one has a *prima facie* obligation to bring about as much good as possible.

In light of these modifications, Ross claims to be able to deal with both the problem of conflicting moral rules and the problem of exceptions. As an example of the problem of conflicting rules, consider the case in which one had a choice between telling the truth, thereby breaking a promise, and keeping a promise by telling a lie. According to Ross, we do not have an obligation either to tell the truth or to keep promises. We only have a *prima facie* obligation to tell the truth and to keep our promises, that is, an obligation to do so unless there are overriding circumstances. In our example, following one rule is more important than following the other, so the presence of the more important rule is the overriding circumstances that frees us from our *prima facie* obligation to follow the less important one. Using this analysis, Ross claims that his system has no problem about conflicting moral rules, and once this problem is solved, the problem about exceptions also disappears. When we are considering a supposed conflict between following a rule and doing what will lead to the best consequences, we are considering, because of (b), a case of two conflicting *prima facie* obligations, and such cases are to be treated as all other cases of conflict of rules.

But has Ross really solved the problem? How are we to tell, in any given case, which *prima facie* obligation outweighs the other? As Harrison points out, Ross has provided no general principle for answering this question. Ross is quite aware of this problem, but he claims that we can rely upon our intuitions about which prima facie obligation is more important. But is this reply satisfactory? Couldn't some general principle be found that would enable us to decide about these difficult cases of conflicting rules and exceptions, cases which pose so much difficulty precisely because we have such unclear intuitions about them? Many philosophers feel that such a general principle is possible and necessary, and have therefore rejected Ross's position because it provides no such principle.

The main alternative to Ross's position is the rule-utilitarian position advocated by Harrison. Whereas the standard utilitarian principle is that an action is right if and only if, among those actions available, it produces the most happiness for all those involved, the rule-utilitarian principle states that an action is right if and only if it is of a sort whose general performance would produce more happiness for all involved than would the general performance of some other sort of action. There is a very big difference between these two principles. While, in evaluating actions, the regular act-utilitarian asks one to consider the consequences of doing that particular action, the rule-utilitarian asks one to consider the consequences of everyone's doing that type of action, of everyone's following the rule "do *x*" (where *x* is a description of the action in question). The rule-utilitarian claims that the very different answers that these questions can have enable his position to avoid the difficulties faced by act-utilitarianism.

In order to see the advantages of rule-utilitarianism, it is helpful to begin by considering the obligation to vote for the candidate who seems most qualified. The act-utilitarian could not explain this obligation, since one vote, because it makes no difference to the outcome of the election, could not produce any human happiness. But the rule-utilitarian can explain this obligation. More human happiness would be produced if everyone voted for the most qualified candidate than if everyone didn't vote, or voted for some other candidate. Therefore, voting for the candidate who seems best is an instance of general performance of a type of action that would maximize human happiness. I therefore have, on rule-utilitarian grounds, an obligation to vote.

How does the rule-utilitarian deal with our most fundamental problem, the problem of exceptions? In particular, can he avoid agreeing with the seemingly incorrect act-utilitarian principle that one ought to break a moral rule as long as the consequences are even slightly better than the consequences of keeping it? Harrison claims that rule-utilitarianism can handle this problem as well. As he points out, the rule-utilitarian always asks us to consider what would happen if everyone did a certain type of action. Consider the question of breaking a promise in order to produce a little additional human happiness. The consequences of everyone's doing that sort of thing would be disastrous, since the whole practice of promising, which helps promote a great deal of human happiness, would be seriously weakened. Since we would be better off if everyone didn't break promises, one should not, as a general rule, break one's promise. The situation is very different if we consider the much rarer case in which a significant gain in human happiness will come about if one breaks one's promise. Since there aren't many cases of this type, and the practice of promising will not be seriously weakened if such promises are broken, we would be better off if everyone did break promises in these cases. In this way, says Harrison, rule-utilitarianism allows in the case of promises, and presumably in other cases as well, for some exceptions to a moral rule.

It is easy to see, in light of the above, why so many philosophers have viewed rule-utilitarianism as an attractive compromise between the extremes of deontological and teleological morality. There are, nevertheless, several important criticisms of this position. J. J. C. Smart argues that rule-utilitarianism involves a superstitious rule worship. After all, says Smart, even if it would be best if people in general followed the rule, "do x," it would be silly for me to do x in a particular case if doing y would lead to more happiness for all concerned in that case. Therefore, says Smart, since ethics is the study of the rational way to act, and not of what we think about morality, we should disregard our intuitions about exceptions and, in agreement with the act-utilitarian, always do the action that will lead to the most good.

Although Professor Strang does not deal explicitly with Smart's argument, one can nevertheless view his paper as a possible reply to it. Strang is concerned with showing why, under certain circumstances, one should be concerned with the consequences of everyone's doing a certain action, and not merely with the consequences of doing that action oneself. The central thesis involves considerations of fairness. If Strang's thesis is correct, it may serve as the basis for a reply to Smart's claim that rule-utilitarianism involves a superstitious rule worship.

Smart, in arguing for act-utilitarianism, stands in opposition to most writers on ethics who agree that both Kantian deontologism and Sidgwickian act-utilitarianism are mistaken. But many philosophers who believe that some compromise position is needed nevertheless feel that Harrison's rule-utilitarianism is not the correct compromise. One such philosopher is R. Brandt. Brandt's objection to Harrison's rule-utilitarianism is that it avoids none of the objections to act-utilitarianism. Indeed, argues Brandt, act-utilitarianism and rule-utilitarianism have the same implications about what is right and what is wrong, so any objections to the former must be objections to the latter as well.

At first glance, Brandt's claim seems strange. Didn't we see before that some actions are right (wrong) on act-utilitarian grounds but wrong (right) on rule-utilitarian grounds? So there must be a difference between the implications of act-utilitarianism and rule-utilitarianism. Brandt's reply is that the arguments used to draw this distinction were mistaken. What action is such that its general performance would lead to the best consequences for all concerned? Surely, it is everyone's doing in a particular case that action which will lead to the best consequences for all concerned. So everyone, according to Harrison's version of rule-utilitarianism, ought to do what will lead to the best consequences in a particular case, that is, everyone should act just as an act-utilitarian says he should.

Brandt is convinced, however, that there is a version of rule-utilitarianism that does have implications different from act-utilitarianism, and is a plausible compromise position. According to this version of rule-utilitarianism, an action is right if and only if it conforms with that learnable set of rules, the recognition of which as morally binding by everyone in the society of the agent (except for the retention by individuals of already formed and decided

moral convictions) would maximize intrinsic value. The point behind this formula is that we ought to act, not in accordance with
the rules whose observance would maximize human happiness, but
the rules which would be best for people, given their limitations,
to recognize and try to follow. Brandt attempts to show that this
version of rule-utilitarianism does offer a plausible account of our
moral obligations.

The reader will have to decide for himself which, if any, of the
various positions we have been considering answers the question of
what to do when our moral rules conflict with our views about what
will lead to the best consequences. But I think that one thing has
become clear in our discussion: this type of problem raises fundamental issues about the nature of right and wrong, and there will
be many cases in which we cannot know how to act until we resolve
these fundamental issues.

IMMANUEL KANT

Morality Based Upon Categorical Imperatives

... Unless we deny that the notion of morality has any truth or reference to any possible object, we must admit that its law must be valid, not merely for men, but for all *rational creatures generally,* not merely under certain contingent conditions or with exceptions, but *with absolute necessity,* then it is clear that no experience could enable us to infer even the possibility of such apodictic laws. For with what right could we bring into unbounded respect as a universal precept for every rational nature that which perhaps holds only under the contingent conditions of humanity? Or how could laws of the determination of *our* will be regarded as laws of the determination of the will of rational beings generally, and for us only as such, if they were merely empirical, and did not take their origin wholly *à priori* from pure but practical reason?

Nor could anything be more fatal to morality than that we should wish to derive it from examples. For every example of it that is set before me must be first itself tested by principles of morality, whether it is worthy to serve as an original example, that is, as a pattern, but by no means can it authoritatively furnish the conception of morality. Even the Holy One of the Gospels must first be

* From Section 2 of Immanuel Kant's *Fundamental Principles of the Metaphysic of Morals,* trans. T. K. Abbott (London: Longmans, Green, & Co., Ltd., 1873).

compared with our ideal of moral perfection before we can recognize Him as such; and so He says of Himself, "Why call ye Me [whom you see] good; none is good [the model of good] but God only [whom ye do not see]?" But whence have we the conception of God as the supreme good? Simply from the *idea* of moral perfection, which reason frames *à priori*, and connects inseparably with the notion of a free will. Imitation finds no place at all in morality, and examples serve only for encouragement, that is, they put beyond doubt the feasibility of what the law commands, they make visible that which the practical rule expresses more generally, but they can never authorize us to set aside the true original which lies in reason, and to guide ourselves by examples.

If then there is no genuine supreme principle of morality but what must rest simply on pure reason, independent on all experience, I think it is not necessary even to put the question, whether it is good to exhibit these concepts in their generality (*in abstracto*) as they are established *à priori* along with the principles belonging to them, if our knowledge is to be distinguished from the *vulgar,* and to be called philosophical. In our times indeed this might perhaps be necessary; for if we collected votes, whether pure rational knowledge separated from everything empirical, that is to say, metaphysic of morals, or whether popular practical philosophy is to be preferred, it is easy to guess which side would preponderate.

This descending to popular notions is certainly very commendable, if the ascent to the principles of pure reason has first taken place and been satisfactorily accomplished. This implies that we first *found* Ethics on Metaphysics, and then, when it is firmly established, procure a *hearing* for it by giving it a popular character. But it is quite absurd to try to be popular in the first inquiry, on which the soundness of the principles depends. It is not only that this proceeding can never lay claim to the very rare merit of a true *philosophical popularity,* since there is no art in being intelligible if one renounces all thoroughness of insight; but also it produces a disgusting medley of compiled observations and half-reasoned principles. Shallow pates enjoy this because it can be used for everyday chat, but the sagacious find in it only confusion, and being unsatisfied and unable to help themselves, they turn away their eyes, while philosophers, who see quite well through this delusion, are little listened to when they call men off for a time from this pretended popularity, in order that they might be rightfully popular after they have attained a definite insight.

We need only look at the attempts of moralists in that favourite fashion, and we shall find at one time the special constitution of human nature (including, however, the idea of a rational nature generally), at one time perfection, at another happiness, here moral sense, there fear of God, a little of this, and a little of that, in marvellous mixture, without its occurring to them to ask whether the principles of morality are to be sought in the knowledge of human nature at all (which we can have only from experience) ; and, if this is not so, if these principles are to be found altogether *à priori* free from everything empirical, in pure rational concepts only, and nowhere else, not even in the smallest degree; then rather to adopt the method of making this a separate inquiry, as pure practical philosophy, or (if one may use a name so decried) as metaphysic of morals,[1] to bring it by itself to completeness, and to require the public, which wishes for popular treatment, to await the issue of this undertaking.

Such a metaphysic of morals, completely isolated, not mixed with any anthropology, theology, physics, or hyperphysics, and still less with occult qualities (which we might call *hypophysical)*, is not only an indispensable substratum of all sound theoretical knowledge of duties, but is at the same time a desideratum of the highest importance to the actual fulfilment of their precepts. For the pure conception of duty, unmixed with any foreign addition of empirical attractions, and, in a word, the conception of the moral law, exercises on the human heart, by way of reason alone (which first becomes aware with this that it can of itself be practical), an influence so much more powerful than all other springs[2] which may be

[1] Just as pure mathematics are distinguished from applied, pure logic from applied, so if we choose we may also distinguish pure philosophy of morals (metaphysic) from applied (*viz.*, applied to human nature). By this designation we are also at once reminded that moral principles are not based on properties of human nature, but must subsist *à priori* of themselves, while from such principles practical rules must be capable of being deduced for every rational nature, and accordingly for that of man.

[2] I have a letter from the late excellent Sulzer, in which he asks me what can be the reason that moral instruction, although containing much that is convincing for the reason, yet accomplishes so little? My answer was postponed in

derived from the field of experience, that in the consciousness of its worth, it despises the latter, and can by degrees become their master; whereas a mixed ethics, compounded partly of motives drawn from feelings and inclinations, and partly also of conceptions of reason, must make the mind waver between motives which cannot be brought under any principle, which lead to good only by mere accident, and very often also to evil.

From what has been said, it is clear that all moral conceptions have their seat and origin completely *à priori* in the reason, and that, moreover, in the commonest reason just as truly as in that which is in the highest degree speculative; that they cannot be obtained by abstraction from any empirical, and therefore merely contingent knowledge; that it is just this purity of their origin that makes them worthy to serve as our supreme practical principle, and that just in proportion as we add anything empirical, we detract from their genuine influence, and from the absolute value of actions; that it is not only of the greatest necessity, in a purely speculative point of view, but is also of the greatest practical importance, to derive these notions and laws from pure reason, to present them pure and unmixed, and even to determine the compass of this practical or pure rational knowledge, that is, to determine the whole faculty of pure practical reason; and, in doing so, we must not make its principles dependent on the particular nature of human reason, though in speculative philosophy this may be permitted, or may even at times be necessary; but since moral laws ought to hold good for every rational creature, we must derive them from the general concept of a rational being. In this way, although for its *application* to man morality has need of anthropology, yet,

---

order that I might make it complete. But it is simply this, that the teachers themselves have not got their own notions clear, and when they endeavour to make up for this by raking up motives of moral goodness from every quarter, trying to make their physic right strong, they spoil it. For the commonest understanding shows that if we imagine, on the one hand, an act of honesty done with steadfast mind, apart from every view to advantage of any kind in this world or another, and even under the greatest temptations of necessity or allurement, and on the other hand, a similar act which was affected, in however low a degree, by a foreign motive, the former leaves far behind and eclipses the second; it elevates the soul, and inspires the wish to be able to act in like manner oneself. Even moderately young children feel this impression, and one should never represent duties to them in any other light.

in the first instance, we must treat it independently as pure philosophy, that is, as metaphysic, complete in itself (a thing which in
such distinct branches of science is easily done); knowing well that
unless we are in possession of this, it would not only be vain to
determine the moral element of duty in right actions for purposes
of speculative criticism, but it would be impossible to base morals
on their genuine principles, even for common practical purposes,
especially of moral instruction, so as to produce pure moral dispositions, and to engraft them on men's minds to the promotion of the
greatest possible good in the world.

But in order that in this study we may not merely advance by
the natural steps from the common moral judgment (in this case
very worthy of respect) to the philosophical, as has been already
done, but also from a popular philosophy, which goes no further
than it can reach by groping with the help of examples, to metaphysic (which does not allow itself to be checked by anything empirical, and as it must measure the whole extent of this kind of
rational knowledge, goes as far as ideal conceptions, where even
examples fail us), we must follow and clearly describe the practical
faculty of reason, from the general rules of its determination to the
point where the notion of duty springs from it.

Everything in nature works according to laws. Rational beings
alone have the faculty of acting according *to the conception* of laws,
that is, according to principles, that is, have a *will*. Since the deduction of actions from principles requires *reason*, the will is nothing but practical reason. If reason infallibly determines the will,
then the actions of such a being which are recognized as objectively
necessary are subjectively necessary also, that is, the will is a faculty
to choose *that only* which reason independent on inclination recognizes as practically necessary, that is, as good. But if reason of itself
does not sufficiently determine the will, if the latter is subject also
to subjective conditions (particular impulses) which do not always
coincide with the objective conditions; in a word, if the will does
not *in itself* completely accord with reason (which is actually the
case with men), then the actions which objectively are recognized
as necessary are subjectively contingent, and the determination of
such a will according to objective laws is *obligation*, that is to say,
the relation of the objective laws to a will that is not thoroughly

good is conceived as the determination of the will of a rational being by principles of reason, but which the will from its nature does not of necessity follow.

The conception of an objective principle, in so far as it is obligatory for a will, is called a *command* (of reason), and the formula of the command is called an *Imperative*.

All imperatives are expressed by the word *ought* [or *shall*], and thereby indicate the relation of an objective law of reason to a will, which from its subjective constitution is not necessarily determined by it (an obligation). They say that something would be good to do or to forbear, but they say it to a will which does not always do a thing because it is conceived to be good to do it. That is practically *good*, however, which determines the will by means of the conceptions of reason, and consequently not from subjective causes, but objectively, that is on principles which are valid for every rational being as such. It is distinguished from the *pleasant*, as that which influences the will only by means of sensation from merely subjective causes, valid only for the sense of this or that one, and not as a principle of reason, which holds for everyone.[3]

A perfectly good will would therefore be equally subject to objective laws (*viz.*, laws of good), but could not be conceived as *obliged* thereby to act lawfully, because of itself from its subjective constitution it can only be determined by the conception of good. Therefore no imperatives hold for the Divine will, or in general for a *holy* will; *ought* is here out of place, because the volition is already of itself necessarily in unison with the law. Therefore impera-

[3] The dependence of the desires on sensations is called *inclination,* and this accordingly always indicates a *want.* The dependence of a contingently determinable will on principles of reason is called an *interest.* This, therefore, is found only in the case of a dependent will which does not always of itself conform to reason; in the Divine will we cannot conceive any interest. But the human will can also *take an interest* in a thing without therefore acting *from* interest. The former signifies the *practical* interest in the action, the latter the *pathological* in the object of the action. The former indicates only dependence of the will on principles of reason in themselves; the second, dependence on principles of reason for the sake of inclination, reason supplying only the practical rules how the requirement of the inclination may be satisfied. In the first case the action interests me; in the second the object of the action (because it is pleasant to me). We have seen in the first section that in an action done from duty we must look not to the interest in the object, but only to that in the action itself, and in its rational principle (*viz.,* the law).

tives are only formulæ to express the relation of objective laws of all volition to the subjective imperfection of the will of this or that rational being, for example, the human will.

Now all *imperatives* command either *hypothetically* or *categorically*. The former represent the practical necessity of a possible action as means to something else that is willed (or at least which one might possibly will). The categorical imperative would be that which represented an action as necessary of itself without reference to another end, that is, as objectively necessary.

Since every practical law represents a possible action as good, and on this account, for a subject who is practically determinable by reason, necessary, all imperatives are formulæ determining an action which is necessary according to the principle of a will good in some respects. If now the action is good only as a means *to something else*, then the imperative is *hypothetical*; if it is conceived as good *in itself* and consequently as being necessarily the principle of a will which of itself conforms to reason, then it is *categorical*.

Thus the imperative declares what action possible by me would be good, and presents the practical rule in relation to a will which does not forthwith perform an action simply because it is good, whether because the subject does not always know that it is good, or because, even if it know this, yet its maxims might be opposed to the objective principles of practical reason.

Accordingly the hypothetical imperative only says that the action is good for some purpose, *possible* or *actual*. In the first case it is a Problematical, in the second an Assertorial practical principle. The categorical imperative which declares an action to be objectively necessary in itself without reference to any purpose, that is, without any other end, is valid as an Apodictic (practical) principle.

Whatever is possible only by the power of some rational being may also be conceived as a possible purpose of some will, and therefore the principles of action as regards the means necessary to attain some possible purpose are in fact infinitely numerous. All sciences have a practical part, consisting of problems expressing that some end is possible for us, and of imperatives directing how it may be attained. These may, therefore, be called in general imperatives of *skill*. Here there is no question whether the end is rational and good, but only what one must do in order to attain it. The precepts for the physician to make his patient thoroughly healthy, and for a poisoner to ensure certain death, are of equal value in this respect, that each serves to effect its purpose perfectly. Since in early youth it cannot be known what ends are likely to occur to us in the course of life, parents seek to have their children taught a *great many things*, and provide for their *skill* in the use of means for all sorts of arbitrary ends, of none of which can they determine whether it may not perhaps hereafter be an object to their pupil, but which it is at all events *possible* that he might aim at; and this anxiety is so great that they commonly neglect to form and correct their judgment on the value of the things which may be chosen as ends.

There is *one* end, however, which may be assumed to be actually such to all rational beings (so far as imperatives apply to them, *viz.*, as dependent beings), and, therefore, one purpose which they not merely *may* have, but which we may with certainty assume that they all actually *have* by a natural necessity, and this is *happiness*. The hypothetical imperative which expresses the practical necessity of an action as means to the advancement of happiness is Assertorial. We are not to present it as necessary for an uncertain and merely possible purpose, but for a purpose which we may presuppose with certainty and *à priori* in every man, because it belongs to his being. Now skill in the choice of means to his own greatest well-being may be called *prudence*,[4] in the narrowest sense. And thus the imperative which refers to the choice of means to one's own happiness, that is, the precept of prudence, is still always *hypothetical*; the action is not commanded absolutely, but only as means to another purpose.

Finally, there is an imperative which commands a certain conduct immediately, without having as its condition any other purpose to be attained by it. This imperative is *Categorical*. It concerns not the matter of the action, or its intended result, but its form and the

---

[4] The word *prudence* is taken in two senses: in the one it may bear the name of knowledge of the world, in the other that of private prudence. The former is a man's ability to influence others so as to use them for his own purposes. The latter is the sagacity to combine all these purposes for his own lasting benefit. This latter is properly that to which the value even of the former is reduced, and when a man is prudent in the former sense, but not in the latter, we might better say of him that he is clever and cunning, but, on the whole, imprudent.

principle of which it is itself a result; and what is essentially good in it consists in the mental disposition, let the consequence be what it may. This imperative may be called that of *Morality*.

There is a marked distinction also between the volitions on these three sorts of principles in the *dissimilarity* of the obligation of the will. In order to mark this difference more clearly, I think they would be most suitably named in their order if we said they are either *rules* of skill, or *counsels* of prudence, or *commands* (*laws*) of morality. For it is *law* only that involves the conception of an *unconditional* and objective necessity, which is consequently universally valid; and commands are laws which must be obeyed, that is, must be followed, even in opposition to inclination. *Counsels*, indeed, involve necessity, but one which can only hold under a contingent subjective condition, namely, they depend on whether this or that man reckons this or that as part of his happiness; the categorical imperative, on the contrary, is not limited by any condition, and as being absolutely, although practically, necessary, may be quite properly called a command. We might also call the first kind of imperatives *technical* (belonging to art), the second *pragmatic*[5] (to welfare), the third *moral* (belonging to free conduct generally, that is, to morals).

Now arises the question, how are all these imperatives possible? This question does not seek to know how we can conceive the accomplishment of the action which the imperative ordains, but merely how we can conceive the obligation of the will which the imperative expresses. No special explanation is needed to show how an imperative of skill is possible. Whoever wills the end, wills also (so far as reason decides his conduct) the means in his power which are indispensably necessary thereto. This proposition is, as regards the volition, analytical; for, in willing an object as my effect, there is already thought the causality of myself as an acting cause, that is to say, the use of the means; and the imperative educes from the conception of volition of an end the conception of actions

---

[5] It seems to me that the proper signification of the word *pragmatic* may be most accurately defined in this way. For *sanctions* are called pragmatic which flow properly, not from the law of the states as necessary enactments, but from *precaution* for the general welfare. A history is composed pragmatically when it teaches *prudence, i.e.,* instructs the world how it can provide for its interests better, or at least as well as the men of former time.

necessary to this end. Synthetical propositions must no doubt be employed in defining the means to a proposed end; but they do not concern the principle, the act of the will, but the object and its realization. For example, that in order to bisect a line on an unerring principle I must draw from its extremities two intersecting arcs; this no doubt is taught by mathematics only in synthetical propositions; but if I know that it is only by this process that the intended operation can be performed, then to say that if I fully will the operation, I also will the action required for it, is an analytical proposition; for it is one and the same thing to conceive something as an effect which I can produce in a certain way, and to conceive myself as acting in this way.

If it were only equally easy to give a definite conception of happiness, the imperatives of prudence would correspond exactly with those of skill, and would likewise be analytical. For in this case as in that, it could be said, whoever wills the end, wills also (according to the dictate of reason necessarily) the indispensable means thereto which are in his power. But, unfortunately, the notion of happiness is so indefinite that although every man wishes to attain it, yet he never can say definitely and consistently what it is that he really wishes and wills. The reason of this is that all the elements which belong to the notion of happiness are altogether empirical, that is, they must be borrowed from experience, and nevertheless the idea of happiness requires an absolute whole, a maximum of welfare in my present and all future circumstances. Now it is impossible that the most clear-sighted and at the same time most powerful being (supposed finite) should frame to himself a definite conception of what he really wills in this. Does he will riches, how much anxiety, envy, and snares might he not thereby draw upon his shoulders? Does he will knowledge and discernment, perhaps it might prove to be only an eye so much the sharper to show him so much the more fearfully the evils that are now concealed from him, and that cannot be avoided, or to impose more wants on his desires, which already give him concern enough. Would he have long life? Who guarantees to him that it would not be a long misery? Would he at least have health? How often has uneasiness of the body restrained from excesses into which perfect health would have allowed one to fall? And so on. In short, he is unable, on any principle, to determine with certainty what would make him truly happy; because to do so he would need to be omniscient. We cannot therefore act on any definite principles to secure happiness, but only on empirical counsels, for example, of regimen, frugality, courtesy, reserve, and so forth, which experience teaches do, on the average, most promote well-being. Hence it follows that the imperatives of prudence do not, strictly speaking, command at all, that is, they cannot present actions objectively as practically *necessary*; that they are rather to be regarded as counsels (*consilia*) than precepts (*præcepta*) of reason, that the problem to determine certainly and universally what action would promote the happiness of a rational being is completely insoluble, and consequently no imperative respecting it is possible which should, in the strict sense, command to do what makes happy; because happiness is not an ideal of reason but of imagination, resting solely on empirical grounds, and it is vain to expect that these should define an action by which one could attain the totality of a series of consequences which is really endless. This imperative of prudence would, however, be an analytical proposition if we assume that the means to happiness could be certainly assigned; for it is distinguished from the imperative of skill only by this, that in the latter the end is merely possible, in the former it is given; as, however, both only ordain the means to that which we suppose to be willed as an end, it follows that the imperative which ordains the willing of the means to him who wills the end is in both cases analytical. Thus there is no difficulty in regard to the possibility of an imperative of this kind either.

On the other hand, the question, how the imperative of *morality* is possible, is undoubtedly one, the only one, demanding a solution, as this is not at all hypothetical, and the objective necessity which it presents cannot rest on any hypothesis, as is the case with the hypothetical imperatives. Only here we must never leave out of consideration that we *cannot* make out *by any example*, in other words empirically, whether there is such an imperative at all; but it is rather to be feared that all those which seem to be categorical may yet be at bottom hypothetical. For instance, when the precept is: Thou shalt not promise deceitfully; and it is assumed that the necessity of this is not a mere counsel to avoid some other evil, so that it should mean: Thou shalt not make a lying promise, lest if it

become known thou shouldst destroy thy credit; but that an action
of this kind must be regarded as evil in itself, so that the imperative
of the prohibition is categorical; then we cannot show with certainty
in any example that the will was determined merely by the law,
without any other spring of action, although it may appear to be so.
For it is always possible that fear of disgrace, perhaps also obscure
dread of other dangers, may have a secret influence on the will.
Who can prove by experience the nonexistence of a cause when all
that experience tells us is that we do not perceive it? But in such a
case the so-called moral imperative, which as such appears to be
categorical and unconditional, would in reality be only a pragmatic
precept, drawing our attention to our own interests, and merely
teaching us to take these into consideration.

We shall therefore have to investigate *à priori* the possibility of
a categorical imperative, as we have not in this case the advantage
of its reality being given in experience, so that [the elucidation of]
its possibility should be requisite only for its explanation, not for
its establishment. In the meantime it may be discerned beforehand
that the categorical imperative alone has the purport of a practical
law: all the rest may indeed be called *principles* of the will but not
laws, since whatever is only necessary for the attainment of some
arbitrary purpose may be considered as in itself contingent, and we
can at any time be free from the precept if we give up the purpose:
on the contrary, the unconditional command leaves the will no liberty to choose the opposite; consequently it alone carries with it
that necessity which we require in a law.

Secondly, in the case of this categorical imperative or law of
morality, the difficulty (of discerning its possibility) is a very pro-
found one. It is an *à priori* synthetical practical proposition;[6] and
as there is so much difficulty in discerning the possibility of speculative propositions of this kind, it may readily be supposed that the
difficulty will be no less with the practical.

[6] I connect the act with the will without presupposing any condition resulting
from any inclination, but *à priori*, and therefore necessarily (though only objectively, *i.e.* assuming the idea of a reason possessing full power over all subjective motives). This is accordingly a practical proposition which does not
deduce the willing of an action by mere analysis from another already presup-
posed (for we have not such a perfect will), but connects it immediately with
the conception of the will of a rational being, as something not contained in it.

In this problem we will first inquire whether the mere conception of a categorical imperative may not perhaps supply us also with the formula of it, containing the proposition which alone can be a categorical imperative; for even if we know the tenor of such an absolute command, yet how it is possible will require further special and laborious study, which we postpone to the last section.

When I conceive a hypothetical imperative, in general I do not know before hand what it will contain until I am given the condition. But when I conceive a categorical imperative, I know at once what it contains. For as the imperative contains besides the law only the necessity that the maxims[7] shall conform to this law, while the law contains no conditions restricting it, there remains nothing but the general statement that the maxim of the action should conform to a universal law, and it is this conformity alone that the imperative properly represents as necessary.

There is therefore but one categorical imperative, namely, this: *Act only on that maxim whereby thou canst at the same time will that it should become a universal law.*

Now if all imperatives of duty can be deduced from this one imperative as from their principle, then, although it should remain undecided whether what is called duty is not merely a vain notion, yet at least we shall be able to show what we understand by it and what this notion means.

Since the universality of the law according to which effects are produced constitutes what is properly called *nature* in the most general sense (as to form), that is the existence of things so far as it is determined by general laws, the imperative of duty may be expressed thus: *Act as if the maxim of thy action were to become by thy will a universal law of nature.*

We will now enumerate a few duties, adopting the usual division of them into duties to ourselves and to others, and into perfect and imperfect duties.[8]

[7] A *Maxim* is a subjective principle of action, and must be distinguished from the *objective principle,* namely, practical law. The former contains the practical rule set by reason according to the conditions of the subject (often its ignorance or its inclinations), so that it is the principle on which the subject *acts;* but the law is the objective principle valid for every rational being, and is the principle on which it *ought to act* that is an imperative.

[8] It must be noted here that I reserve the division of duties for a future

(1) A man reduced to despair by a series of misfortunes feels wearied of life, but is still so far in possession of his reason that he can ask himself whether it would not be contrary to his duty to himself to take his own life. Now he inquires whether the maxim of his action could become a universal law of nature. His maxim is: From self-love I adopt it as a principle to shorten my life when its longer duration is likely to bring more evil than satisfaction. It is asked then simply whether this principle founded on self-love can become a universal law of nature. Now we see at once that a system of nature of which it should be a law to destroy life by means of the very feeling whose special nature it is to impel to the improvement of life would contradict itself, and therefore could not exist as a system of nature; hence that maxim cannot possibly exist as a universal law of nature, and consequently would be wholly inconsistent with the supreme principle of all duty.

(2) Another finds himself forced by necessity to borrow money. He knows that he will not be able to repay it, but sees also that nothing will be lent to him, unless he promises stoutly to repay it in a definite time. He desires to make this promise, but he has still so much conscience as to ask himself: Is it not unlawful and inconsistent with duty to get out of a difficulty in this way? Suppose, however, that he resolves to do so, then the maxim of his action would be expressed thus: When I think myself in want of money, I will borrow money and promise to repay it, although I know that I never can do so. Now this principle of self-love or of one's own advantage may perhaps be consistent with my whole future welfare; but the question now is, is it right? I change then the suggestion of self-love into a universal law, and state the question thus: How would it be if my maxim were a universal law? Then I see at once that it could never hold as a universal law of nature, but would necessarily contradict itself. For supposing it to be a universal law that everyone when he thinks himself in a difficulty should be able to promise

---

metaphysic of morals; so that I give it here only as an arbitrary one (in order to arrange my examples). For the rest, I understand by a perfect duty one that admits no exception in favour of inclination, and then I have not merely external but also internal perfect duties. This is contrary to the use of the word adopted in the schools; but I do not intend to justify it here, as it is all one for my purpose whether it is admitted or not.

whatever he pleases, with the purpose of not keeping his promise, the promise itself would become impossible, as well as the end that one might have in view in it, since no one would consider that anything was promised to him, but would ridicule all such statements as vain pretences.

(3) A third finds in himself a talent which with the help of some culture might make him a useful man in many respects. But he finds himself in comfortable circumstances, and prefers to indulge in pleasure rather than to take pains in enlarging and improving his happy natural capacities. He asks, however, whether his maxim of neglect of his natural gifts, besides agreeing with his inclination to indulgence, agrees also with what is called duty. He sees then that a system of nature could indeed subsist with such a universal law although men (like the South Sea islanders) should let their talents rest, and resolve to devote their lives merely to idleness, amusement, and propagation of their species—in a word, to enjoyment; but he cannot possibly *will* that this should be a universal law of nature, or be implanted in us as such by a natural instinct. For, as a rational being, he necessarily wills that his faculties be developed, since they serve him, and have been given him, for all sorts of possible purposes.

(4) A fourth, who is in prosperity, while he sees that others have to contend with great wretchedness and that he could help them, thinks: What concern is it of mine? Let everyone be as happy as Heaven pleases, or as he can make himself; I will take nothing from him nor even envy him, only I do not wish to contribute anything to his welfare or to his assistance in distress! Now no doubt if such a mode of thinking were a universal law, the human race might very well subsist, and doubtless even better than in a state in which everyone talks of sympathy and good will, or even takes care occasionally to put it into practice, but, on the other side, also cheats when he can, betrays the rights of men, or otherwise violates them. But although it is possible that a universal law of nature might exist in accordance with that maxim, it is impossible to *will* that such a principle should have the universal validity of a law of nature. For a will which resolved this would contradict itself, inasmuch as many cases might occur in which one would have need of the love and sympathy of others, and in which, by such a law of

nature, sprung from his own will, he would deprive himself of all hope of the aid he desires.

These are a few of the many actual duties, or at least what we regard as such, which obviously fall into two classes on the one principle that we have laid down. We must be *able to will* that a maxim of our action should be a universal law. This is the canon of the moral appreciation of the action generally. Some actions are of such a character that their maxim cannot without contradiction be even *conceived* as a universal law of nature, far from it being possible that we should *will* that it *should* be so. In others this in-trinsic impossibility is not found, but still it is impossible to *will* that their maxim should be raised to the universality of a law of nature, since such a will would contradict itself. It is easily seen that the former violate strict or rigorous (inflexible) duty; the latter only laxer (meritorious) duty. Thus it has been completely shown by these examples how all duties depend as regards the nature of the obligation (not the object of the action) on the same principle.

If now we attend to ourselves on occasion of any transgression of duty, we shall find that we in fact do not will that our maxim should be a universal law, for that is impossible for us; on the con-trary, we will that the opposite should remain a universal law, only we assume the liberty of making an *exception* in our own favour or (just for this time only) in favour of our inclination. Consequently if we considered all cases from one and the same point of view, namely, that of reason, we should find a contradiction in our own will, namely, that a certain principle should be objectively necessary as a universal law, and yet subjectively should not be universal, but admit of exceptions. As, however, we at one moment regard our action from the point of view of a will wholly conformed to reason, and then again look at the same action from the point of view of a will affected by inclination, there is not really any contradiction, but an antagonism of inclination to the precept of reason, whereby the universality of the principle is changed into a mere generality, so that the practical principle of reason shall meet the maxim half way. Now, although this cannot be justified in our own impartial judgment, yet it proves that we do really recognize the validity of the categorical imperative and (with all respect for it) only allow ourselves a few exceptions, which we think unimportant and forced from us.

We have thus established at least this much, that if duty is a conception which is to have any import and real legislative authority for our actions, it can only be expressed in categorical, and not at all in hypothetical imperatives. We have also, which is of great importance, exhibited clearly and definitely for every practical application the content of the categorical imperative, which must contain the principle of all duty if there is such a thing at all.

. . . .

IMMANUEL KANT

On a Supposed Right
to Tell Lies from
Benevolent Motives

In the work called *France*, for the year 1797, Part VI, No. 1, on Political Reactions, by Benjamin Constant, the following passage occurs, page 123:

"The moral principle that it is one's duty to speak the truth, if it were taken singly and unconditionally, would make all society impossible. We have the proof of this in the very direct consequences which have been drawn from this principle by a German philosopher, who goes so far as to affirm that to tell a falsehood to a murderer who asked us whether our friend, of whom he was in pursuit, had not taken refuge in our house, would be a crime." [1]

The French philosopher opposes this principle in the following manner, page 124: "It is a duty to tell the truth. The notion of duty is inseparable from the notion of right. A duty is what in one being corresponds to the right of another. Where there are no rights there are no duties. To tell the truth then is a duty, but only towards him who has a right to the truth. But no man has a right to a truth

---

* From *Kant's Critique of Practical Reason and Other Works on the Theory of Ethics*, trans. T. K. Abbott (London: Longmans, Green & Co., 1873).

[1] "J. D. Michaelis, in Göttingen, propounded the same strange opinion even before Kant. That Kant is the philosopher here referred to, I have been informed by the author of this work himself."—K. F. Cramer.

I hereby admit that I have really said this in some place which I cannot now recollect.—I. Kant.

that injures others." The πρῶτον ψεῦδος here lies in the statement
that *"To tell the truth is a duty, but only towards him who has a
right to the truth."*

It is to be remarked, first, that the expression "to have a right to
the truth" is unmeaning. We should rather say, a man has a right
to his own *truthfulness* (*veracitas*), that is, to subjective truth in
his own person. For to have a right objectively to truth would mean
that as in *meum* and *tuum* generally, it depends on his *will* whether
a given statement shall be true or false, which would produce a
singular logic.

Now, the *first* question is whether a man—in cases where he
cannot avoid answering *yes* or *no*—has the *right* to be untruthful.
The *second* question is whether, in order to prevent a misdeed that
threatens him or some one else, he is not actually bound to be untruthful in a certain statement to which an unjust compulsion forces
him.

Truth in utterances that cannot be avoided is the formal duty of
a man to everyone,[2] however great the disadvantage that may arise
from it to him or any other; and although by making a false statement I do no wrong to him who unjustly compels me to speak, yet I
do wrong to men in general in the most essential point of duty, so
that it may be called a lie (though not in the jurist's sense), that is,
so far as in me lies I cause that declarations in general find no
credit, and hence that all rights founded on contract should lose
their force; and this is a wrong which is done to mankind.

If, then, we define a lie merely as an intentionally false declaration towards another man, we need not add that it must injure
another; as the jurists think proper to put in their definition (*men-
dacium est falsiloquium in praejudicium alterius*). For it always
injures another; if not another individual, yet mankind generally,
since it vitiates the source of justice. This benevolent lie *may*, however, by *accident* (*casus*) become punishable even by civil laws;
and that which escapes liability to punishment only by accident
may be condemned as a wrong even by external laws. For instance,

---

[2] I do not wish here to press this principle so far as to say that "falsehood
is a violation of duty to oneself." For this principle belongs to Ethics, and
here we are speaking only of a duty of justice. Ethics look in this transgression
only to the *worthlessness*, the reproach of which the liar draws on himself.

if you have *by a lie* hindered a man who is even now planning a murder, you are legally responsible for all the consequences. But if you have strictly adhered to the truth, public justice can find no fault with you, be the unforeseen consequence what it may. It is possible that whilst you have honestly answered *yes* to the murderer's question, whether his intended victim is in the house, the latter may have gone out unobserved, and so not have come in the way of the murderer, and the deed therefore have not been done; whereas, if you lied and said he was not in the house, and he had really gone out (though unknown to you) so that the murderer met him as he went, and executed his purpose on him, then you might with justice be accused as the cause of his death. For, if you had spoken the truth as well as you knew it, perhaps the murderer while seeking for his enemy in the house might have been caught by neighbours coming up and the deed been prevented. Whoever then *tells a lie,* however good his intentions may be, must answer for the consequences of it, even before the civil tribunal, and must pay the penalty for them, however unforeseen they may have been; because truthfulness is a duty that must be regarded as the basis of all duties founded on contract, the laws of which would be rendered uncertain and useless if even the least exception to them were admitted.

To be *truthful* (honest) in all declarations is therefore a sacred unconditional command of reason, and not to be limited by any expediency.

M. Constant makes a thoughtful and sound remark on the decrying of such strict principles, which it is alleged lose themselves in impracticable ideas, and are therefore to be rejected (p. 123): "In every case in which a principle proved to be true seems to be inapplicable, it is because we do not know the *middle principle* which contains the medium of its application." He adduces (p. 121) the doctrine of *equality* as the first link forming the social chain (p. 121): "namely, that no man can be bound by any laws except those to the formation of which he has contributed. In a very contracted society this principle may be directly applied and become the ordinary rule without requiring any middle principle. But in a very numerous society we must add a new principle to that which we here state. This middle principle is, that the individuals may contribute to the formation of the laws either in their own person or by *representatives*. Whoever would try to apply the first principle to a numerous society without taking in the middle principle would infallibly bring about its destruction. But this circumstance, which would only show the ignorance or incompetence of the lawgiver, would prove nothing against the principle itself." He concludes (p. 125) thus: "A principle recognized as truth must, therefore, never be abandoned, however obviously danger may seem to be involved in it." (And yet the good man himself abandoned the unconditional principle of veracity on account of the danger to society, because he could not discover any middle principle which would serve to prevent this danger; and, in fact, no such principle is to be interpolated here.)

Retaining the names of the persons as they have been here brought forward, "the French philosopher" confounds the action by which one does harm (*nocet*) to another by telling the truth, the admission of which he cannot avoid, with the action by which he does him *wrong* (*lædit*). It was merely an *accident* (*casus*) that the truth of the statement did harm to the inhabitant of the house; it was not a free *deed* (in the juridical sense). For to admit his right to require another to tell a lie for his benefit would be to admit a claim opposed to all law. Every man has not only a right, but the strictest duty to truthfulness in statements which he cannot avoid, whether they do harm to himself or others. He himself, properly speaking, does not *do* harm to him who suffers thereby; but this harm is *caused* by accident. For the man is not free to choose, since (if he must speak at all) veracity is an unconditional duty. The "German philosopher" will therefore not adopt as his principle the proposition (p. 124): "It is a duty to speak the truth, but only to him who has *a right to the truth,*" first on account of the obscurity of the expression, for truth is not a possession the right to which can be granted to one, and refused to another; and next and chiefly, because the duty of veracity (of which alone we are speaking here) makes no distinction between persons towards whom we have this duty, and towards whom we may be free from it; but is an *unconditional duty* which holds in all circumstances.

Now, in order to proceed from a *metaphysic* of *Right* (which abstracts from all conditions of experience) to a principle of *politics* (which applies these notions to cases of experience), and by means of this to the solution of a problem of the latter in accordance with the general principle of right, the philosopher will enunciate: (1) An *Axiom*, that is, an apodictically certain proposition, which follows directly from the definition of external right (harmony of the *freedom* of each with the freedom of all by a universal law). (2) A *Postulate* of external public *law* as the united will of all on the principle of *equality*, without which there could not exist the freedom of all. (3) A *Problem*; how it is to be arranged that harmony may be maintained in a society, however large, on principles of freedom and equality (namely, by means of a representative system); and this will then become a principle of the *political system*, the establishment and arrangement of which will contain enactments which, drawn from practical knowledge of men, have in view only the mechanism of administration of justice, and how this is to be suitably carried out. Justice must never be accommodated to the political system, but always the political system to justice.

"A principle recognized as true (I add, recognized *à priori*, and therefore apodictic) must never be abandoned, however obviously danger may seem to be involved in it," says the author. Only here we must not understand the danger of *doing harm* (accidentally), but of *doing wrong*; and this would happen if the duty of veracity, which is quite unconditional, and constitutes the supreme condition of justice in utterances, were made conditional and subordinate to other considerations; and, although by a certain lie I in fact do no wrong to any person, yet I infringe the principle of justice in regard to all indispensably necessary statements *generally* (I do wrong formally, though not materially); and this is much worse than to commit an injustice to any individual, because such a deed does not presuppose any principle leading to it in the subject. The man who, when asked whether in the statement he is about to make he intends to speak truth or not, does not receive the question with indignation at the suspicion thus expressed towards him that he might be a liar, but who asks permission first to consider possible exceptions, is already a liar (*in potentia*), since he shows that he does not recognize veracity as a duty in itself, but reserves exceptions from a rule which in its nature does not admit of exceptions, since to do so would be self-contradictory.

All practical principles of justice must contain strict truths, and the principles here called middle principles can only contain the closer definition of their application to actual cases (according to the rules of politics), and never exceptions from them, since exceptions destroy the universality, on account of which alone they bear the name of principles.

HENRY SIDGWICK

Utilitarian Morality

THE MEANING OF UTILITARIANISM

§ 1. The term *Utilitarianism* is, at the present day, in common use, and is supposed to designate a doctrine or method with which we are all familiar. But on closer examination, it appears to be applied to several distinct theories, having no necessary connexion with one another, and not even referring to the same subject matter. It will be well, therefore, to define, as carefully as possible, the doctrine that is to be denoted by the term in the present Book: at the same time distinguishing this from other doctrines to which usage would allow the name to be applied, and indicating, so far as seems necessary, its relation to these.

By Utilitarianism is here meant the ethical theory, that the conduct which, under any given circumstances, is objectively right, is that which will produce the greatest amount of happiness on the whole; that is, taking into account all whose happiness is affected by the conduct. It would tend to clearness if we might call this principle, and the method based upon it, by some such name as "Universalistic Hedonism": and I have therefore sometimes ventured to use this term, in spite of its cumbrousness.

The first doctrine from which it seems necessary to distinguish

* From Chapters 1 and 3 of Book IV in Henry Sidgwick's *Methods of Ethics,* 4th ed. (The Macmillan Company: 1890).

this, is the *Egoistic Hedonism* expounded and discussed in Book II of this treatise. The difference, however, between the propositions (1) that each ought to seek his own happiness, and (2) that each ought to seek the happiness of all, is so obvious and glaring, that instead of dwelling upon it we seem rather called upon to explain how the two ever came to be confounded, or in any way included under one notion. This question and the general relation between the two doctrines were briefly discussed in a former chapter.[1] Among other points it was there noticed that the confusion between these two ethical theories was partly assisted by the confusion with both of the psychological theory that in voluntary actions every agent does, universally or normally, seek his own individual happiness or pleasure. Now there seems to be no *necessary* connexion between this latter proposition and any ethical theory: but in so far as there is a natural tendency to pass from psychological to ethical Hedonism, the transition must be—at least primarily—to the Egoistic phase of the latter. For clearly, from the fact that every one actually does seek his own happiness we cannot conclude, as an immediate and obvious inference, that he ought to seek the happiness of other people.[2]

Nor, again, is Utilitarianism, as an ethical doctrine, necessarily connected with the psychological theory that the moral sentiments are derived, by "association of ideas" or otherwise, from experiences of the nonmoral pleasures and pains resulting to the agent or to others from different kinds of conduct. An Intuitionist might accept this theory, so far as it is capable of scientific proof, and still hold that these moral sentiments, being found in our present consciousness as independent impulses, ought to possess the authority that they seem to claim over the more primary desires and aversions from which they have sprung: and an Egoist on the other hand might fully admit the altruistic element of the derivation, and still hold that these and all other impulses (including even Universal Benevolence) are properly under the rule of Rational Self-love: and

[1] Book I, Chap. vi. It may be worth while to notice, that in Mill's well-known treatise on Utilitarianism this confusion, though expressly deprecated, is to some extent encouraged by the author's treatment of the subject.

[2] I have already criticised (Book III, Chap. xiii) the mode in which Mill attempts to exhibit this inference.

that it is really only reasonable to gratify them in so far as we may expect to find our private happiness in such gratification. In short, what is often called the "utilitarian" theory of the origin of the moral sentiments cannot by itself provide a proof of the ethical doctrine to which I in this treatise restrict the term Utilitarianism. I shall, however, hereafter try to show that this psychological theory has an important though subordinate place in the establishment of Ethical Utilitarianism.[3]

Finally, the doctrine that Universal Happiness is the ultimate *standard* must not be understood to imply that Universal Benevolence is the only right or always best *motive* of action. For, as we have before observed, it is not necessary that the end which gives the criterion of rightness should always be the end at which we consciously aim: and if experience shows that the general happiness will be more satisfactorily attained if men frequently act from other motives than pure universal philanthropy, it is obvious that these other motives are reasonably to be preferred on Utilitarian principles.

§ 2. Let us now examine the principle itself somewhat closer. I have already attempted (Book II, Chap. i) to render the notion of Greatest Happiness as clear and definite as possible; and the results there obtained are of course as applicable to the discussion of Universalistic as to that of Egoistic Hedonism. We shall understand, then, that by Greatest Happiness is meant the greatest possible surplus of pleasure over pain, the pain being conceived as balanced against an equal amount of pleasure, so that the two contrasted amounts annihilate each other for purposes of ethical calculation. And of course, here as before, the assumption is involved that all pleasures included in our calculation are capable of being compared quantitatively with one another and with all pains; that every such feeling has a certain intensive quantity, positive or negative (or, perhaps, zero), in respect of its desirableness, and that this quantity may be to some extent known: so that each may be at least roughly weighed in ideal scales against any other. This assumption is involved in the very notion of Maximum Happiness; as the attempt to make "as great as possible" a sum of ele-

[3] Cf. *post*, Chap. iv.

ments not quantitatively commensurable would be a mathematical absurdity. Therefore whatever weight is to be attached to the objections brought against this assumption (which was discussed in Chap. iii of Book II) must of course tell against the present method.

We have next to consider who the "all" are, whose happiness is to be taken into account. Are we to extend our concern to all the beings capable of pleasure and pain whose feelings are affected by our conduct? or are we to confine our view to human happiness? The former view is the one adopted by Bentham and Mill, and (I believe) by the Utilitarian school generally: and is obviously most in accordance with the universality that is characteristic of their principle. It is the Good *Universal,* interpreted and defined as "happiness" or "pleasure," at which a Utilitarian considers it his duty to aim: and it seems arbitrary and unreasonable to exclude from the end, as so conceived, any pleasure of any sentient being.

It may be said that by giving this extension to the notion, we considerably increase the scientific difficulties of the hedonistic comparison, which have already been pointed out (Book II, Chap. iii): for if it be difficult to compare the pleasures and pains of other men accurately with our own, a comparison of either with the pleasures and pains of brutes is obviously still more obscure. Still, the difficulty is at least not greater for Utilitarians than it is for any other moralists who recoil from the paradox of disregarding altogether the pleasures and pains of brutes. But even if we limit our attention to human beings, the extent of the subjects of happiness is not yet quite determinate. In the first place, it may be asked, how far we are to consider the interests of posterity when they seem to conflict with those of existing human beings. It seems, however, clear that the time at which a man exists cannot affect the value of his happiness from a universal point of view; and that the interests of posterity must concern a Utilitarian as much as those of his contemporaries, except in so far as the effect of his actions on posterity—and even the existence of human beings to be affected—must necessarily be more uncertain. But a further question arises when we consider that we can to some extent influence the number of future human (or sentient) beings. We have to ask how, on Utilitarian principles, this influence is to be exercised. Here I shall assume that, for human beings generally, life on the average yields a positive balance of pleasure over pain. This has been denied by thoughtful persons: but the denial seems to me clearly opposed to the common experience of mankind, as expressed in their commonly accepted principles of action. The great majority of men, in the great majority of conditions under which human life is lived, certainly act as if death were one of the worst of evils, for themselves and for those whom they love: and the administration of criminal justice proceeds on a similar assumption.[4]

Assuming, then, that the average happiness of human beings is a positive quantity, it seems clear that, supposing the average happiness enjoyed remains undiminished, Utilitarianism directs us to make the number enjoying it as great as possible. But if we foresee as possible that an increase in numbers will be accompanied by a decrease in average happiness or *vice versa,* a point arises which has not only never been formally noticed, but which seems to have been substantially overlooked by many Utilitarians. For if we take Utilitarianism to prescribe, as the ultimate end of action, happiness on the whole, and not any individual's happiness, unless considered as an element of the whole, it would follow that, if the additional population enjoy on the whole positive happiness, we ought to weigh the amount of happiness gained by the extra number against the amount lost by the remainder. So that, strictly conceived, the point up to which, on Utilitarian principles, population ought to be encouraged to increase, is not that at which average happiness

[4] Those who held the opposite opinion appear generally to assume that the appetites and desires which are the mainspring of ordinary human action are in themselves painful: a view entirely contrary to my own experience, and, I believe, to the common experience of mankind. See Chap. iv, § 2 of Book I. So far as their argument is not a development of this psychological error, any plausibility it has seems to me to be obtained by dwelling onesidedly on the annoyances and disappointments undoubtedly incident to normal human life, and on the exceptional sufferings of small minorities of the human race, or perhaps of most men during small portions of their lives.

The reader who wishes to see the paradoxical results of pessimistic utilitarianism seriously worked out by a thoughtful and suggestive writer, may refer to Professor Macmillan's book on the *Promotion of General Happiness* (Swan Sonnenschein and Co. 1890). The author considers that "the philosophical world is pretty equally divided between optimists and pessimists," and his own judgment on the question at issue between the two schools appears to be held in suspense.

is the greatest possible—as appears to be often assumed by political economists of the school of Malthus—but that at which the product formed by multiplying the number of persons living into the amount of average happiness reaches its maximum.

It may be well here to make a remark which has a wide application in Utilitarian discussion. The conclusion just given wears a certain air of absurdity to the view of Common Sense; because its show of exactness is grotesquely incongruous with our consciousness of the inevitable inexactness of all such calculations in actual practice. But, that our practical Utilitarian reasonings must necessarily be rough, is no reason for not making them as accurate as the case admits; and we shall be more likely to succeed in this if we keep before our mind as distinctly as possible the strict type of the calculation that we should have to make, if all the relevant considerations could be estimated with mathematical precision.

There is one more point that remains to be noticed. It is evident that there may be many different ways of distributing the same quantum of happiness among the same number of persons; in order, therefore, that the Utilitarian criterion of right conduct may be as complete as possible, we ought to know which of these ways is to be preferred. This question is often ignored in expositions of Utilitarianism. It has perhaps seemed somewhat idle, as suggesting a purely abstract and theoretical perplexity, that could have no practical exemplification; and no doubt, if all the consequences of actions were capable of being estimated and summed up with mathematical precision, we should probably never find the excess of pleasure over pain exactly equal in the case of two competing alternatives of conduct. But the very indefiniteness of all hedonistic calculations, which was sufficiently shown in Book II, renders it by no means unlikely that there may be no *cognisable* difference between the quantities of happiness involved in two sets of consequences respectively; the more rough our estimates necessarily are, the less likely we shall be to come to any clear decision between two apparently balanced alternatives. In all such cases, therefore, it becomes practically important to ask whether any mode of distributing a given quantum of happiness is better than any other. Now the Utilitarian formula seems to supply no answer to this question: at least we have to supplement the principle of seeking the greatest happiness on the whole by some principle of Just or Right distribution of this happiness. The principle which most Utilitarians have either tacitly or expressly adopted is that of pure equality— as given in Bentham's formula, "everybody to count for one, and nobody for more than one." And this principle seems the only one which does not need a special justification; for, as we saw, it must be reasonable to treat any one man in the same way as any other, if there be no reason apparent for treating him differently.[5]

. . . .

RELATION OF UTILITARIANISM TO THE MORALITY OF COMMON SENSE

§ 1. It has been before observed (Book I, Chap. vi) that the two sides of the double relation in which Utilitarianism stands to the Morality of Common Sense have been respectively prominent at two different periods in the history of English ethical thought. Since Bentham we have been chiefly familiar with the negative or aggressive aspect of the Utilitarian doctrine. But when Cumberland, replying to Hobbes, put forward the general tendency of the received moral rules to promote the "common Good [6] of all Rationals" his aim was simply Conservative: it never occurs to him to consider whether these rules as commonly formulated are in any way imperfect, and whether there are any discrepancies between such common moral opinions and the conclusions of Rational Benevolence. So in Shaftesbury's system the "Moral" or "Reflex Sense" is supposed to be always pleased with that "balance" of the affections which tends to the good or happiness of the whole, and displeased with

[5] It should be observed that the question here is as too the distribution of *Happiness*, not the *means of happiness*. If more happiness on the whole is produced by giving the same means of happiness to B rather than to A, it is an obvious and incontrovertible deduction from the Utilitarian principle that it ought to be given to B, whatever inequality in the distribution of the *means* of happiness this may involve.

[6] It ought to be observed that Cumberland does not adopt a hedonistic interpretation of Good. Still, I have followed Hallam in regarding him as the founder of English Utilitarianism: since it seems to have been by a gradual and half-unconscious process that "Good" came to have the definitely hedonistic meaning which it has implicitly in Shaftesbury's system, and explicitly in that of Hume.

the opposite. In Hume's treatise this coincidence is drawn out more in detail, and with a more definite assertion that the perception of utility[7] (or the reverse) is in each case the source of the moral likings (or aversions) which are excited in us by different qualities of human character and conduct. And we may observe that the most penetrating among Hume's contemporary critics, Adam Smith, admits unreservedly the objective coincidence of Rightness or Approvedness and Utility: though he maintains, in opposition to Hume, that "it is not the view of this utility or hurtfulness, which is either the first or the principal source of our approbation or disapprobation." After stating Hume's theory that "no qualities of the mind are approved of as virtuous, but such as are useful or agreeable either to the person himself or to others, and no qualities are disapproved of as vicious but such as have a contrary tendency"; he remarks that "Nature seems indeed to have so happily adjusted our sentiments of approbation and disapprobation to the conveniency both of the individual and of the society, that after the strictest examination it will be found, I believe, that this is universally the case."

And no one can read Hume's *Inquiry into the First Principles of Morals* without being convinced of this at least, that if a list were drawn up of the qualities of character and conduct that are directly or indirectly productive of pleasure to ourselves or to others, it would include all that are commonly known as virtues. Whatever be the origin of our notion of moral goodness or excellence, there is no doubt that "Utility" is a general characteristic of the dispositions to which we apply it: and that, so far, the Morality of Common Sense may be truly represented as at least unconsciously Utilitarian. But it may still be objected, that this coincidence is merely general and qualitative, and that it breaks down when we attempt

[7] I should point out that Hume uses "utility" in a narrower sense than that which Bentham gave it, and one more in accordance with the usage of ordinary language. He distinguishes the "useful" from the "immediately agreeable": so that while recognising "utility" as the main ground of our moral approbation of the more important virtues, he holds that there are other elements of personal merit which we approve because they are "immediately agreeable," either to the person possessed of them or to others. It appears, however, more convenient to use the word in the wider sense in which it has been current since Bentham.

to draw it out in detail, with the quantitative precison which Bentham introduced into the discussion. And no doubt there is a great difference between the assertion that virtue is always productive of happiness, and the assertion that the right action is under all circumstances that which will produce the greatest possible happiness on the whole. But it must be borne in mind that Utilitarianism is not concerned to prove the absolute coincidence in results of the Intuitional and Utilitarian methods. Indeed, if it could succeed in proving as much as this, its success would be almost fatal to its practical claims; as the adoption of the Utilitarian principle would then become a matter of complete indifference. Utilitarians are rather called upon to show a natural transition from the Morality of Common Sense to Utilitarianism, somewhat like the transition in special branches of practice from trained instinct and empirical rules to the technical method that embodies and applies the conclusions of science: so that Utilitarianism may be presented as the scientifically complete and systematically reflective form of that regulation of conduct, which through the whole course of human history has always tended substantially in the same direction. For this purpose it is not necessary to prove that existing moral rules are *more* conducive to the general happiness than any others: but only to point out in each case some manifest felicific tendency which they possess.

Hume's dissertation, however, incidentally exhibits much more than a simple and general harmony between the moral sentiments with which we commonly regard actions and their foreseen pleasurable and painful consequences. And, in fact, the Utilitarian argument cannot be fairly judged unless we take fully into account the cumulative force which it derives from the complex character of the coincidence between Utilitarianism and Common Sense.

It may be shown, I think, that the Utilitarian estimate of consequences not only supports broadly the current moral rules, but also sustains their generally received limitations and qualifications: that, again, it explains anomalies in the Morality of Common Sense, which from any other point of view must seem unsatisfactory to the reflective intellect; and moreover, where the current formula is not sufficiently precise for the guidance of conduct, while at the same time difficulties and perplexities arise in the attempt to give it additional precision, the Utilitarian method solves these difficulties and perplexities in general accordance with the vague instincts of Common Sense, and is naturally appealed to for such solution in ordinary moral discussions. It may be shown further, that it not only supports the generally received view of the relative importance of different duties, but is also naturally called in as arbiter, where rules commonly regarded as coordinate come into conflict: that, again, when the same rule is interpreted somewhat differently by different persons, each naturally supports his view by urging its Utility, however strongly he may maintain the rule to be self-evident and known *a priori*: that where we meet with marked diversity of moral opinion on any point, in the same age and country, we commonly find manifest and impressive utilitarian reasons on both sides: and that finally the remarkable discrepancies found in comparing the moral codes of different ages and countries are for the most part strikingly correlated to differences in the effects of actions on happiness, or in men's foresight of, or concern for, such effects. Most of these points are noticed by Hume, though in a somewhat casual and fragmentary way, and many of them have been incidentally illustrated in the course of the examination of Common Sense Morality, with which we were occupied in the preceding Book. But considering the importance of the present question, it may be well to exhibit in systematic detail the cumulative argument which has just been summed up, even at the risk of repeating to some extent the results previously given.

. . . .

§ 3. Let us then examine first the group of virtues and duties discussed in Book III, Chap. iv, under the head of Benevolence. As regards the general conception of the duty, there is, I think, no divergence that we need consider between the Intuitional and Utilitarian systems. For though Benevolence would perhaps be more commonly defined as a disposition to promote the Good of one's fellow creatures, rather than their Happiness (as definitely understood by Utilitarians); still, as the chief element in the common notion of good (besides happiness) is moral good or Virtue,[8] if we

[8] Book III, Chap. iv, § 1.

can show that the other virtues are—speaking broadly—all qualities conducive to the happiness of the agent himself or of others, it is evident that Benevolence, whether it prompts us to promote the virtue of others or their happiness, will aim directly or indirectly at the Utilitarian end.[9]

Nor, further, does the comprehensive range which Utilitarians give to Benevolence, in stating as their ultimate end the greatest happiness of all sentient beings, seem to be really opposed to Common Sense; for in so far as certain Intuitional moralists restrict the scope of the direct duty of Benevolence to human beings, and regard our duties to brute animals as merely indirect and derived "from the duty of Self-culture," they rather than their Utilitarian opponents appear paradoxical. And if, in laying down that each agent is to consider all other happiness as equally important with his own, Utilitarianism seems to go beyond the standard of duty commonly prescribed under the head of Benevolence, it yet can scarcely be said to conflict with Common Sense on this point. For the practical application of this theoretical impartiality of Utilitarianism is limited to several important considerations. In the first place, generally speaking, each man is better able to provide for his own happiness than for that of other persons, from his more intimate knowledge of his own desires and needs, and his greater opportunities of gratifying them. And besides, it is under the stimulus of self-interest that the active energies of most men are most easily and thoroughly drawn out: and if this were removed, general happiness would be diminished by a serious loss of those means of happiness which are obtained by labour; and also, to some extent, by the diminution of the labour itself. For these reasons it would not under actual circumstances promote the universal happiness if each man were to concern himself with the happiness of others as much as with his own. While if I consider the duty abstractly and ideally, even Common Sense morality seems to bid me "love my neighbour as myself."

It might indeed be plausibly objected, on the other hand, that under the notions of Generosity, Self-sacrifice, and so forth, Common Sense praises (though it does not prescribe as obligatory) a sup-

---

[9] It will be seen that I do not here assume in their full breadth the conclusions of Chap. xiv of the preceding Book.

pression of egoism beyond what Utilitarianism approves: for we perhaps admire as virtuous a man who gives up his own happiness for another's sake, even when the happiness that he confers is clearly less than that which he resigns, so that there is a diminution of happiness on the whole. But (1) it seems very doubtful whether we do altogether approve such conduct when the disproportion between the sacrifice and the benefit is obvious and striking: and (2) a spectator is often unable to judge whether happiness is lost on the whole, as (a) he cannot tell how far he who makes the sacrifice is compensated by sympathetic and moral pleasure, and (b) the remoter felicific consequences flowing from the moral effects of such a sacrifice on the agent and on others have to be taken into account: while (3) even if there be a loss in the particular case, still our admiration of self-sacrifice will admit of a certain Utilitarian justification, because such conduct shows a disposition far above the average in its general tendency to promote happiness, and it is perhaps this disposition that we admire rather than the particular act.

It has been said,[10] however, that the special claims and duties belonging to special relations, by which each man is connected with a few out of the whole number of human beings, are expressly ignored by the rigid impartiality of the Utilitarian formula: and hence that, though Utilitarianism and Common Sense may agree in the proposition that all right action is conducive to the happiness of some one or other, and so far beneficent, still they are irreconcileably divergent on the radical question of the *distribution* of beneficence.

Here, however, it seems that even fair-minded opponents have scarcely understood the Utilitarian position. They have attacked Bentham's well-known formula, "every man to count for one, nobody for more than one," on the ground that the general happiness will be best attained by inequality in the distribution of each one's services. But so far as it is clear that it will be best attained in this way, Utilitarianism will necessarily prescribe this way of aiming at it; and Bentham's dictum must be understood merely as making the conception of the ultimate end precise—laying down

---

[10] Cf. J. Grote, *An Examination of the Utilitarian Philosophy*, Chap. v.

that one person's happiness is to be counted for as much as another's (supposed equal in degree) as an element of the general happiness— not as directly prescribing the rules of conduct by which this end will be best attained. And the reasons why it is, generally speaking, conducive to the general happiness that each individual should dis- tribute his beneficence in the channels marked out by commonly recognised ties and claims, are tolerably obvious.

For first, in the chief relations discussed in Chap. iv of Book III —the domestic, and those constituted by consanguinity, friendship, previous kindnesses, and special needs—the services which Common Sense prescribes as duties are commonly prompted by natural affec- tion, while at the same time they tend to develop and sustain such affection. Now the subsistence of benevolent affections among human beings is itself an important means to the Utilitarian end, because (as Shaftesbury and his followers forcibly urged) the most intense and highly valued of our pleasures are derived from such affections; for both the emotion itself is highly pleasurable, and it imparts this quality to the activities which it prompts and sustains, and the happiness thus produced is continually enhanced by the sympathetic echo of the pleasures conferred on others. And again, where genuine affection subsists, the practical objections to spon- taneous beneficence, which were before noticed, are much dimin- ished in force. For such affection tends to be reciprocated, and the kindnesses which are its outcome and expression commonly win a requital of affection: and in so far as this is the case, they have less tendency to weaken the springs of activity in the person benefited; and may even strengthen them by exciting other sources of energy than the egoistic—personal affection, and gratitude, and the desire to deserve love, and the desire to imitate beneficence. And hence it has been often observed that the injurious effects of almsgiving are at least much diminished if the alms are bestowed with unaffected sympathy and kindliness, and in such a way as to elicit a genuine response of gratitude. And further, the beneficence that springs from affection is less likely to be frustrated from defect of knowledge: for not only are we powerfully stimulated to study the real con- ditions of the happiness of those whom we love, but also such study is rendered more effective from the sympathy which naturally ac- companies affection.

On these grounds the Utilitarian will evidently approve of the cultivation of affection and the performance of affectionate services. It may be said, however, that what we ought to approve is not so much affection for special individuals, but rather a feeling more universal in its scope—charity, philanthropy, or (as it has been called) the "Enthusiasm of Humanity." And certainly all special affections tend occasionally to come into conflict with the principle of promoting the general happiness: and Utilitarianism must therefore prescribe such a culture of the feelings as will, so far as possible, counteract this tendency. But it seems that most persons are only capable of strong affections towards a few human beings in certain close relations, especially the domestic: and that if these were suppressed, what they would feel towards their fellow creatures generally would be, as Aristotle says, "but a watery kindness" and a very feeble counterpoise to self-love: so that such specialised affections as the present organisation of society normally produces afford the best means of developing in most persons a more extended benevolence, to the degree to which they are capable of feeling it. Besides, each person is for the most part, from limitation either of power or knowledge, not in a position to do much good to more than a very small number of persons; it therefore seems, on this ground alone, desirable that his chief benevolent impulses should be correspondingly limited.

And this leads us to consider, secondly, the reasons why, affection apart, it is conducive to the general happiness that special claims to services should be commonly recognised as attaching to special relations; so as to modify that impartiality in the distribution of beneficence which Utilitarianism *prima facie* inculcates. For clearness' sake it seems best to take this argument separately, though it cannot easily be divided from the former one, because the services in question are often such as cannot so well be rendered without affection. In such cases, as we saw,[11] Common Sense regards the affection itself as a duty, in so far as it is capable of being cultivated: but still prescribes the performance of the services even if the affection be unhappily absent. Indeed we may properly consider the services to which we are commonly prompted by the domestic affec-

---

[11] Book III, Chap. iv, § 1.

tions, and also those to which we are moved by gratitude and pity, as an integral part of the system of mutual aid by which the normal life and happiness of society is maintained, under existing circumstances; being an indispensable supplement to the still more essential services which are definitely prescribed by Law, or rendered on commercial terms as a part of an express bargain. As political economists have explained, the means of happiness are immensely increased by that complex system of cooperation which has been gradually organised among civilised men: and while it is thought that under such a system it will be generally best on the whole to let each individual exchange such services as he is disposed to render for such return as he can obtain for them by free contract, still there are many large exceptions to this general principle. Of these the most important is constituted by the case of children. It is necessary for the well-being of mankind that in each generation children should be produced in adequate numbers, neither too many nor too few; and that, as they cannot be left to provide for themselves, they should be adequately nourished and protected during the period of infancy; and further, that they should be carefully trained in good habits, intellectual, moral, and physical: and it is commonly believed that the best or even the only known means of attaining these ends in even a tolerable degree is afforded by the existing institution of the Family, resting as it does on a basis of legal and moral rules combined. For Law fixes a minimum of mutual services and draws the broad outlines of behaviour for the different members of the family, imposing[12] on the parents lifelong union and complete mutual fidelity and the duty of providing for their children the necessaries of life up to a certain age; in return for which it gives them the control of their children for the same period, and sometimes lays on the latter the burden of supporting their parents when aged and destitute: so that Morality, in inculcating a completer harmony of interests and an ampler interchange of kindnesses, is merely filling in the outlines drawn by Law. We found, however, in attempting to formulate the different domestic duties as recognised by Common Sense, that there seemed to be in most

[12] Strictly speaking, of course, the Law of modern states does not enforce this, but only refuses to recognise connubial contracts of any other kind: but the social effect is substantially the same.

cases a large vague margin with respect to which general agreement could not be affirmed, and which, in fact, forms an arena for continual disputes. But we have now to observe that it is just this margin which reveals most clearly the latent Utilitarianism of common moral opinion: for when the question is once raised as to the precise mutual duties, for example, of husbands and wives, or of parents and children, each disputant commonly supports his view by a forecast of the effects on human happiness to be expected from the general establishment of any proposed rule; this seems to be the standard to which the matter is, by common consent, referred.

Similarly the claim to services that arises out of special need (which natural sympathy moves us to recognise) may obviously be rested on an utilitarian basis: indeed the proper fulfilment of this duty seems so important to the well-being of society, that it has in modern civilised communities generally been brought to some extent within the sphere of Governmental action. We noticed that the main utilitarian reason why it is not right for every rich man to distribute his superfluous wealth among the poor, is that the happiness of all is on the whole most promoted by maintaining in adults generally (except married women), the expectation that each will be thrown on his own resources for the supply of his own wants. But if I am made aware that, owing to a sudden calamity that could not have been foreseen, another's resources are manifestly inadequate to protect him from pain or serious discomfort, the case is altered; my theoretical obligation to consider his happiness as much as my own becomes at once practical; and I am bound to make as much effort to relieve him as will not entail a greater loss of happiness to myself or others. If, however, the calamity is one which might have been foreseen and averted by proper care, my duty becomes more doubtful: for then by relieving him I seem to be in danger of encouraging improvidence in others. In such a case a Utilitarian has to weigh this indirect evil against the direct good of removing pain and distress: and it is now more and more generally recognised that the question of providing for the destitute has to be treated as a utilitarian problem of which these are the elements— whether we are considering the minimum that should be secured to them by law, or the proper supplementary action of private charity.

Poverty, however, is not the only case in which it is conducive to the general happiness that one man should render unbought services to another. In any condition or calling a man may find himself unable to ward off some evil, or to realise some legitimate or worthy end, without assistance of such kind as he cannot purchase on the ordinary commercial terms—assistance which, on the one hand, will have no bad effect on the receiver, from the exceptional nature of the emergency while at the same time it may not be burdensome to the giver. Here, again, some jurists have thought that where the service to be rendered is great, and the burden of rendering it very slight, it might properly be made matter of legal obligation: so that, for example, if I could save a man from drowning by merely holding out a hand, I should be legally punishable if I omitted the act. But, however this may be, the moral rule condemning the refusal of aid in such emergencies is obviously conducive to the general happiness.

Further, besides these—so to say—*accidentally* unbought services, there are some for which there is normally no market price; such as counsel and assistance in the intimate perplexities of life, which one is only willing to receive from genuine friends. It much promotes the general happiness that such services should be generally rendered. On this ground, as well as through the emotional pleasures which directly spring from it, we perceive Friendship to be an important means to the Utilitarian end. At the same time we feel that the charm of Friendship is lost if the flow of emotion is not spontaneous and unforced. The combination of these two views seems to be exactly represented by the sympathy that is not quite admiration with which Common Sense regards all close and strong affections; and the regret that is not quite disapproval with which it contemplates their decay.

In all cases where it is conducive to the general happiness that unbought services should be rendered, Gratitude (if we mean by this a settled disposition to repay the benefit in whatever way one can on a fitting opportunity) is enjoined by Utilitarianism no less than by Common Sense; for experience would lead us to expect that no kind of onerous services will be adequately rendered unless there is a general disposition to requite them. In fact we may say that a general understanding that all services which it is expedient that

A should render to *B* will be in some way repaid by *B,* is a natural
supplement of the more definite contracts by which the main part
of the great social interchange of services is arranged. Indeed the
one kind of requital merges in the other, and no sharp line can be
drawn between the two: we cannot always say distinctly whether the
requital of a benefit is a pure act of gratitude or the fulfilment of
a tacit understanding.[13] There is, however, a certain difficulty in
this view of gratitude as analogous to the fulfilment of a bargain.
For it may be said that of the services peculiar to friendship dis-
interestedness is an indispensable characteristic; and that in all
cases benefits conferred without expectation of reward have a peculiar excellence, and are indeed peculiarly adapted to arouse
gratitude; but if they are conferred in expectation of such gratitude,
they lose this excellence; and yet, again, it would be very difficult
to treat as a friend one from whom gratitude was not expected.
This seems, at first sight, an inextricable entanglement: but here,
as in other cases, an apparent ethical contradiction is found to
reduce itself to a psychological complexity. For most of our actions
are done from several different motives, either coexisting or succeeding one another in rapid alternation: thus a man may have a
perfectly disinterested desire to benefit another, and one which
might possibly prevail over all conflicting motives if all hope of
requital were cut off, and yet it may be well that this generous
impulse should be sustained by a vague trust that requital will
not be withheld. And in fact the apparent puzzle really affords
another illustration of the latent Utilitarianism of Common Sense.
For, on the one hand, Utilitarianism prescribes that we should
render services whenever it is conducive to the general happiness to
do so, which may often be the case without taking into account the
gain to oneself which would result from their requital: and on the
other hand, since we may infer from the actual selfishness of
average men that such services would not be adequately rendered
without expectation of requital, it is also conducive to the general
happiness that men should recognise a moral obligation to repay
them.

[13] Sometimes such unbargained requital is even legally obligatory: as when
children are bound to repay the care spent on them by supporting their parents
in decrepitude.

We have discussed only the most conspicuous of the duties of affection: but it is probably obvious that similar reasonings would apply in the case of the others.

In all such cases there are three distinct lines of argument which tend to show that the commonly received view of special claims and duties arising out of special relations, though *prima facie* opposed to the impartial universality of the Utilitarian principle, is really maintained by a well-considered application of that principle. First, morality is here in a manner protecting the normal channels and courses of natural benevolent affections; and the development of such affections is of the highest importance to human happiness, both as a direct source of pleasure, and as an indispensable preparation for a more enlarged "altruism." And again, the mere fact that such affections are normal, causes an expectation of the services that are their natural expression; and the disappointment of such expectations is inevitably painful. While finally, apart from these considerations, we can show in each case strong utilitarian reasons why, generally speaking, services should be rendered to the persons commonly recognised as having such claims rather than to others.

We have to observe, in conclusion, that the difficulties which we found in the way of determining by the Intuitional method the limits and the relative importance of these duties are reduced in the Utilitarian system, to difficulties of hedonistic comparison. For each of the preceding arguments has shown us different kinds of pleasures gained and pains averted by the fulfilment of the claims in question. There are, first, those which the service claimed would directly promote or avert: secondly, there is the pain and secondary harm of disappointed expectation, if the service be not rendered: thirdly, we have to reckon the various pleasures connected with the exercise of natural benevolent affections, especially when reciprocated, including the indirect effects on the agent's character of maintaining such affections. All these different pleasures and pains combine differently, and with almost infinite variation as circumstances vary, into utilitarian reasons for each of the claims in question; none of these reasons being absolute and conclusive, but each having its own weight, while liable to be outweighed by others.

. . . .

§ 5. The duty of Truth-speaking is sometimes taken as a striking instance of a moral rule not resting on a Utilitarian basis. But a careful study of the qualifications with which the common opinion of mankind actually inculcates this duty seems to lead us to an opposite result: for not only is the general utility of truth-speaking so manifest as to need no proof, but wherever this utility seems to be absent, or outweighed by particular bad consequences, we find that Common Sense at least hesitates to enforce the rule. For example, if a man be pursuing criminal ends, it is *prima facie* injurious to the community that he should be aided in his pursuit by being able to rely on the assertions of others. Here, then, deception is *prima facie* legitimate as a protection against crime: though when we consider the bad effects on habit, and through example, of even a single act of unveracity, the case is seen to be, on Utilitarian principles, doubtful: and this is just the view of Common Sense. Again, though it is generally a man's interest to know the truth, there are exceptional cases in which it is injurious to him—as when an invalid hears bad news—and here, too, Common Sense is disposed to suspend the rule. Again, we found it difficult to define exactly wherein Veracity consists; for we may either require truth in the spoken words, or in the inferences which the speaker foresees will be drawn from them, or in both. Perfect Candour, no doubt, would require it in both: but in the various circumstances where this seems inexpedient, we often find Common Sense at least half-willing to dispense with one or other part of the double obligation. Thus we found a respectable school of thinkers maintaining that a religious truth may properly be communicated by means of a historical fiction: and, on the other hand, the unsuitability of perfect frankness to our existing social relations is recognised in the common rules of politeness, which impose on us not unfrequently the necessity of suppressing truths and suggesting falsehoods. I would not say that in any of these cases Common Sense pronounces quite decidedly in favour of unveracity: but then neither is Utilitarianism decided, as the utility of maintaining a general habit of truth-speaking is so great, that it is not easy to prove it to be clearly outweighed by even strong special reasons for violating the rule.

Yet it may be worth while to point out how the different views as to the legitimacy of Malevolent impulses, out of which we found it hard to frame a consistent doctrine for Common Sense, exactly correspond to different forecasts of the consequences of gratifying such impulses. *Prima facie,* the desire to injure any one in particular is inconsistent with a deliberate purpose of benefiting as much as possible people in general; accordingly, we find that what I may call Superficial Common Sense passes a sweeping condemnation on such desires. But a study of the actual facts of society shows that resentment plays an important part in that repression of injuries which is necessary to social well-being; accordingly, the reflective moralist shrinks from excluding it altogether. It is evident, however, that personal ill will is a very dangerous means to the general happiness: for its direct end is the exact opposite of happiness; and though the realisation of this end may in certain cases be the least of two evils, still the impulse if encouraged is likely to prompt to the infliction of pain beyond the limits of just punishment, and to have an injurious reaction on the character of the angry person. Accordingly, the moralist is disposed to prescribe that indignation be directed always against acts, and not against persons; and if indignation so restricted would be efficient in repressing injuries, this would seem to be the state of mind most conducive to the general happiness. But it is doubtful whether average human nature is capable of maintaining this distinction, and whether, if it could be maintained, the more refined aversion would by itself be sufficiently efficacious: accordingly, Common Sense hesitates to condemn personal ill will against wrongdoers—even if it includes a desire of malevolent satisfaction.

Finally, it is easy to show that Temperance, Self-control, and what are called the Self-regarding virtues generally, are "useful" to the individual who possesses them: and if it is not quite clear, in the view of Common Sense, to what end that regulation and government of appetites and passions, which moralists have so much inculcated and admired, is to be directed; at least there seems no obstacle in the way of our defining this end as Happiness. And even in the ascetic extreme of Self-control, which has sometimes led to the repudiation of sensual pleasures as radically bad, we may trace an unconscious Utilitarianism. For the ascetic condemnation has always been chiefly directed against those pleasures, in respect of which men are especially liable to commit excesses dangerous to health;

and free indulgence in which, even when it keeps clear of injury to health, is thought to interfere with the development of other faculties and susceptibilities which are important sources of happiness.

. . . .

§ 7. The preceding survey has supplied us with several illustrations of the manner in which Utilitarianism is normally introduced as a method for deciding between different conflicting claims, in cases where common sense leaves their relative importance obscure —as, for example, between the different duties of the affections, and the different principles which analysis shows to be involved in our common conception of Justice—and we have also noticed how, when a dispute is raised as to the precise scope and definition of any current moral rule, the effects of different acceptations of the rule on general happiness or social well-being are commonly regarded as the ultimate grounds on which the dispute is to be decided. In fact these two arguments practically run into one; for it is generally a conflict between maxims that impresses men with the need of giving each a precise definition. It may be urged that the consequences to which reference is commonly made in such cases are rather effects on "social well-being" than on "general happiness" as understood by Utilitarians; and that the two notions ought not to be identified. I grant this: but in the last chapter of the preceding Book I have tried to show that Common Sense is unconsciously utilitarian in its practical determination of those very elements in the notion of Ultimate Good or Well-being which at first sight least admit of a hedonistic interpretation. We may now observe that this hypothesis of "Unconscious Utilitarianism" explains the different relative importance attached to particular virtues by different classes of human beings, and the different emphasis with which the same virtue is inculcated on these different classes by mankind generally. For such differences ordinarily correspond to variations—real or apparent—in the Utilitarian importance of the virtues under different circumstances. Thus we have noticed the greater stress laid on chastity in women than in men: courage, on the other hand, is more valued in the latter, as they are more called upon to cope energetically with sudden and severe dangers. And for similar reasons a soldier is expected to show a higher degree of courage than, for example, a priest. Again, though we esteem candour and scrupulous sincerity in most persons, we scarcely look for them in a diplomatist who has to conceal secrets, nor do we expect that a tradesman in describing his goods should frankly point out their defects to his customers.

Finally, when we compare the different moral codes of different ages and countries, we see that the discrepancies among them correspond, at least to a great extent, to differences either in the actual effects of actions on happiness, or in the extent to which such effects are generally foreseen—or regarded as important—by the men among whom the codes are maintained. Several instances of this have already been noticed: and the general fact, which has been much dwelt upon by Utilitarian writers, is also admitted and even emphasised by their opponents. Thus Dugald Stewart[14] lays stress on the extent to which the moral judgments of mankind have been modified by "the diversity in their physical circumsances," the "unequal degrees of civilisation which they have attained," and "their unequal measures of knowledge or of capacity." He points out, for instance, that theft is regarded as a very venial offence in the South Sea Islanders, because little or no labour is there required to support life; that the lending of money for interest is commonly reprehended in societies where commerce is imperfectly developed, because the "usurer" in such communities is commonly in the odious position of wringing a gain out of the hard necessities of his fellows; and that where the legal arrangements for punishing crime are imperfect, private murder is either justified or regarded very leniently. Many other examples might be added to these if it were needful. But I conceive that few persons who have studied the subject will deny that there is a certain degree of correlation between the variations in the moral code from age to age, and the variations in the real or perceived effects on general happiness of actions prescribed or forbidden by the code. And in proportion as the apprehension of consequences becomes more comprehensive and exact, we may trace not only change in the moral code handed down from age to age, but progress in the direction of a closer approximation to a

[14] *Active and Moral Powers*, Book II, Chap. iii.

perfectly enlightened Utilitarianism. Only we must distinctly notice another important factor in the progress, which Stewart has not mentioned: the extension, namely, of the capacity for sympathy in an average member of the community. The imperfection of earlier moral codes is at least as much due to defectiveness of sympathy as of intelligence; often, no doubt, the ruder man did not perceive the effects of his conduct on others; but often, again, he perceived them more or less, but felt little or no concern about them. Thus it happens that changes in the conscience of a community often correspond to changes in the extent and degree of the sensitiveness of an average member of it to the feelings of others. Of this the moral development historically worked out under the influence of Christianity affords familiar illustrations.[15]

I am not maintaining that this correlation between the development of current morality and the changes in the consequences of conduct as sympathetically forecast, is perfect and exact. On the contrary—as I shall have occasion to point out in the next chapter —the history of morality shows us many evidences of what, from the Utilitarian point of view, appear to be partial aberrations of the moral sense. But even in these instances we can often discover a germ of unconscious Utilitarianism; the aberration is often only an exaggeration of an obviously useful sentiment, or the extension of it by mistaken analogy to cases to which it does not properly apply, or perhaps the survival of a sentiment which once was useful but has now ceased to be so.

Further, it must be observed that I have carefully abstained from asserting that the perception of the rightness of any kind of conduct has always—or even ordinarily—been derived by conscious inference from a perception of consequent advantages. This hypothesis is naturally suggested by such a survey as the preceding; but the evidence of history hardly seems to me to support it: since, as we

[15] Among definite changes in the current morality of the Græco-Roman civilised world, which are to be attributed mainly if not entirely to the extension and intensification of sympathy due to Christianity, the following may be especially noted: (1) the severe condemnation and final suppression of the practice of exposing infants; (2) effective abhorrence of the barbarism of gladiatorial combats; (3) immediate moral mitigation of slavery, and a strong encouragement of emancipation; (4) great extension of the eleemosynary provision made for the sick and poor.

retrace the development of ethical thought, the Utilitarian basis of current morality, which I have endeavoured to exhibit in the present chapter, seems to be rather less than more distinctly apprehended by the common moral consciousness. Thus, for example, Aristotle sees that the sphere of the Virtue of Courage (ἀνδρεία), as recognised by the Common Sense of Greece, is restricted to dangers in war: and we can now explain this limitation by a reference to the utilitarian importance of this kind of courage, at a period of history when the individual's happiness was bound up more completely than it now is with the welfare of his state, while the very existence of the latter was more frequently imperilled by hostile invasions: but this explanation lies quite beyond the range of Aristotle's own reflection. The origin of our moral notions and sentiments lies hid in those obscure regions of hypothetical history where conjecture has free scope: but we do not find that, as our retrospect approaches the borders of this realm, the conscious connexion in men's minds between accepted moral rules and foreseen effects on general happiness becomes more clearly traceable. The admiration felt by early man for beauties or excellences of character seems to have been as direct and unreflective as his admiration of any other beauty: and the stringency of law and custom in primitive times presents itself as sanctioned by the evils which divine displeasure will supernaturally inflict on their violators, rather than by even a rude and vague forecast of the natural bad consequences of nonobservance. It is therefore not as the mode of regulating conduct with which mankind began, but rather as that to which we can now see that human development has been always tending, as the adult and not the germinal form of Morality, that Utilitarianism may most reasonably claim the acceptance of Common Sense.

. . . .

SIR DAVID ROSS

What Makes Right Acts Right?

~~~~~~

The real point at issue between hedonism and utilitarianism on the one hand and their opponents on the other is not whether "right" means "productive of so and so"; for it cannot with any plausibility be maintained that it does. The point at issue is that to which we now pass, namely, whether there is any general character which makes right acts right, and if so, what it is. Among the main historical attempts to state a single characteristic of all right actions which is the foundation of their rightness are those made by egoism and utilitarianism. But I do not propose to discuss these, not because the subject is unimportant, but because it has been dealt with so often and so well already, and because there has come to be so much agreement among moral philosophers that neither of these theories is satisfactory. A much more attractive theory has been put forward by Professor Moore: that what makes actions right is that they are productive of more *good* than could have been produced by any other action open to the agent.[1]

This theory is in fact the culmination of all the attempts to base rightness on productivity of some sort of result. The first form this attempt takes is the attempt to base rightness on conduciveness

* From pp. 16–47 of Sir David Ross's *The Right and the Good*. Reprinted by permission of the Clarendon Press, Oxford.

[1] I take the theory which, as I have tried to show, seems to be put forward in *Ethics* rather than the earlier and less plausible theory put forward in *Principia Ethica*.

to the advantage or pleasure of the agent. This theory comes to grief over the fact, which stares us in the face, that a great part of duty consists in an observance of the rights and a furtherance of the interests of others, whatever the cost to ourselves may be. Plato and others may be right in holding that a regard for the rights of others never in the long run involves a loss of happiness for the agent, that "the just life profits a man." But this, even if true, is irrelevant to the rightness of the act. As soon as a man does an action *because* he thinks he will promote his own interests thereby, he is acting not from a sense of its rightness but from self-interest.

To the egoistic theory hedonistic utilitarianism supplies a much-needed amendment. It points out correctly that the fact that a certain pleasure will be enjoyed by the agent is no reason why he *ought* to bring it into being rather than an equal or greater pleasure to be enjoyed by another, though, human nature being what it is, it makes it not unlikely that he *will* try to bring it into being. But hedonistic utilitarianism in its turn needs a correction. On reflection it seems clear that pleasure is not the only thing in life that we think good in itself, that for instance we think the possession of a good character, or an intelligent understanding of the world, as good or better. A great advance is made by the substitution of "productive of the greatest good" for "productive of the greatest pleasure."

Not only is this theory more attractive than hedonistic utilitarianism, but its logical relation to that theory is such that the latter could not be true unless *it* were true, while it might be true though hedonistic utilitarianism were not. It is in fact one of the logical bases of hedonistic utilitarianism. For the view that what produces the maximum pleasure is right has for its bases the views (1) that what produces the maximum good is right, and (2) that pleasure is the only thing good in itself. If they were not assuming that what produces the maximum *good* is right, the utilitarians' attempt to show that pleasure is the only thing good in itself, which is in fact the point they take most pains to establish, would have been quite irrelevant to their attempt to prove that only what produces the maximum *pleasure* is right. If, therefore, it can be shown that productivity of the maximum good is not what makes all right actions right, we shall *a fortiori* have refuted hedonistic utilitarianism.

When a plain man fulfils a promise because he thinks he ought to do so, it seems clear that he does so with no thought of its total consequences, still less with any opinion that these are likely to be the best possible. He thinks in fact much more of the past than of the future. What makes him think it right to act in a certain way is the fact that he has promised to do so—that and, usually, nothing more. That his act will produce the best possible consequences is not his reason for calling it right. What lends colour to the theory we are examining, then, is not the actions (which form probably a great majority of our actions) in which some such reflection as "I have promised" is the only reason we give ourselves for thinking a certain action right, but the exceptional cases in which the consequences of fulfilling a promise (for instance) would be so disastrous to others that we judge it right not to do so. It must of course be admitted that such cases exist. If I have promised to meet a friend at a particular time for some trivial purpose, I should certainly think myself justified in breaking my engagement if by doing so I could prevent a serious accident or bring relief to the victims of one. And the supporters of the view we are examining hold that my thinking so is due to my thinking that I shall bring more good into existence by the one action than by the other. A different account may, however, be given of the matter, an account which will, I believe, show itself to be the true one. It may be said that besides the duty of fulfilling promises I have and recognize a duty of relieving distress,[2] and that when I think it right to do the latter at the cost of not doing the former, it is not because I think I shall produce more good thereby but because I think it the duty which is in the circumstances more of a duty. This account surely corresponds much more closely with what we really think in such a situation. If, so far as I can see, I could bring equal amounts of good into being by fulfilling my promise and by helping some one to whom I had made no promise, I should not hesitate to regard the former as my duty. Yet on the view that what is right is right because it is productive of the most good I should not so regard it.

There are two theories, each in its way simple, that offer a solution of such cases of conscience. One is the view of Kant, that there

---

[2] These are not strictly speaking duties, but things that tend to be our duty, or *prima facie* duties. Cf. pp. 66–67.

are certain duties of perfect obligation, such as those of fulfilling promises, of paying debts, of telling the truth, which admit of no exception whatever in favour of duties of imperfect obligation, such as that of relieving distress. The other is the view of, for instance, Professor Moore and Dr. Rashdall, that there is only the duty of producing good, and that all "conflicts of duties" should be resolved by asking "by which action will most good be produced?" But it is more important that our theory fit the facts than that it be simple, and the account we have given above corresponds (it seems to me) better than either of the simpler theories with what we really think, namely, that normally promise-keeping, for example, should come before benevolence, but that when and only when the good to be produced by the benevolent act is very great and the promise comparatively trivial, the act of benevolence becomes our duty.

In fact the theory of "ideal utilitarianism," if I may for brevity refer so to the theory of Professor Moore, seems to simplify unduly our relations to our fellows. It says, in effect, that the only morally significant relation in which my neighbours stand to me is that of being possible beneficiaries by my action.[3] They do stand in this relation to me, and this relation is morally significant. But they may also stand to me in the relation of promisee to promiser, of creditor to debtor, of wife to husband, of child to parent, of friend to friend, of fellow countryman to fellow countryman, and the like; and each of these relations is the foundation of a *prima facie* duty, which is more or less incumbent on me according to the circumstances of the case. When I am in a situation, as perhaps I always am, in which more than one of these *prima facie* duties is incumbent on me, what I have to do is to study the situation as fully as I can until I form the considered opinion (it is never more) that in the circumstances one of them is more incumbent than any other; then I am bound to think that to do this *prima facie* duty is my duty *sans phrase* in the situation.

I suggest "*prima facie* duty" or "conditional duty" as a brief way

[3] Some will think it, apart from considerations, a sufficient refutation of this view to point out that I also stand in that relation to myself, so that for this view the distinction of oneself from others is morally insignificant.

of referring to the characteristic (quite distinct from that of being a duty proper) which an act has, in virtue of being of a certain kind (*e.g.* the keeping of a promise), of being an act which would be a duty proper if it were not at the same time of another kind which is morally significant. Whether an act is a duty proper or actual duty depends on *all* the morally significant kinds it is an instance of. The phrase *"prima facie* duty" must be apologized for, since (1) it suggests that what we are speaking of is a certain kind of duty, whereas it is in fact not a duty, but something related in a special way to duty. Strictly speaking, we want not a phrase in which duty is qualified by an adjective, but a separate noun. (2) *"Prima" facie* suggests that one is speaking only of an appearance which a moral situation presents at first sight, and which may turn out to be illusory; whereas what I am speaking of is an objective fact involved in the nature of the situation, or more strictly in an element of its nature, though not, as duty proper does, arising from its *whole* nature. I can, however, think of no term which fully meets the case. "Claim" has been suggested by Professor Prichard. The word "claim" has the advantage of being quite a familiar one in this connexion, and it seems to cover much of the ground. It would be quite natural to say, "a person to whom I have made a promise has a claim on me," and also, "a person whose distress I could relieve (at the cost of breaking the promise) has a claim on me." But (1) while "claim" is appropriate from *their* point of view, we want a word to express the corresponding fact from the agent's point of view—the fact of his being subject to claims that can be made against him; and ordinary language provides us with no such correlative to "claim." And (2) (what is more important) "claim" seems inevitably to suggest two persons, one of whom might make a claim on the other; and while this covers the ground of social duty, it is inappropriate in the case of that important part of duty which is the duty of cultivating a certain kind of character in oneself. It would be artificial, I think, and at any rate metaphorical, to say that one's character has a claim on oneself.

There is nothing arbitrary about these *prima facie* duties. Each rests on a definite circumstance which cannot seriously be held to be without moral significance. Of *prima facie* duties I suggest, without claiming completeness or finality for it, the following division.[4]

(1) Some duties rest on previous acts of my own. These duties seem to include two kinds, (a) those resting on a promise or what may fairly be called an implicit promise, such as the implicit undertaking not to tell lies which seems to be implied in the act of entering into conversation (at any rate by civilized men), or of writing books that purport to be history and not fiction. These may be called the duties of fidelity. (b) Those resting on a previous wrongful act. These may be called the duties of reparation. (2) Some rest on previous acts of other men, that is, services done by them to me. These may be loosely described as the duties of gratitude.[5] (3) Some rest on the fact or possibility of a distribution of pleasure or happiness (or of the means thereto) which is not in accordance with the merit of the persons concerned; in such cases there arises a duty to upset or prevent such a distribution. These are the duties of justice. (4) Some rest on the mere fact that there are other beings in the world whose condition we can make better in respect of virtue, or of intelligence, or of pleasure. These are the duties of beneficence. (5) Some rest on the fact that we can improve our own condition in respect of virtue or of intelligence. These are the duties of self-improvement. (6) I think that we should distinguish from (4) the duties that may be summed up under the title of "not injuring others." No doubt to injure others is incidentally to fail to do them good; but it seem to me clear that nonmaleficence is apprehended as a duty distinct from that of beneficence, and as a duty of a more stringent character. It will be noticed that this alone among the types of duty has been stated in a negative way. An attempt might no

---

[4] I should make it plain at this stage that I am *assuming* the correctness of some of our main convictions as to *prima facie* duties, or, more strictly, am claiming that we *know* them to be true. To me it seems as self-evident as anything could be, that to make a promise, for instance, is to create a moral claim on us in someone else. Many readers will perhaps say that they do *not* know this to be true. If so, I certainly cannot prove it to them; I can only ask them to reflect again, in the hope that they will ultimately agree that they also know it to be true. The main moral convictions of the plain man seem to me to be, not opinions which it is for philosophy to prove or disprove, but knowledge from the start; and in my own case I seem to find little difficulty in distinguishing these essential convictions from other moral convictions which I also have, which are merely fallible opinions based on an imperfect study of the working for good or evil of certain institutions or types of action.

[5] For a needed correction of this statement, cf. p. 69.

doubt be made to state this duty, like the others, in a positive way. It might be said that it is really the duty to prevent ourselves from acting either from an inclination to harm others or from an inclination to seek our own pleasure, in doing which we should incidentally harm them. But on reflection it seems clear that the primary duty here is the duty not to harm others, this being a duty whether or not we have an inclination that if followed would lead to our harming them; and that when we have such an inclination the primary duty not to harm others gives rise to a consequential duty to resist the inclination. The recognition of this duty of nonmaleficence is the first step on the way to the recognition of the duty of beneficence; and that accounts for the prominence of the commands "thou shalt not kill," "thou shalt not commit adultery," "thou shalt not steal," "thou shalt not bear false witness," is so early a code as the Decalogue. But even when we have come to recognize the duty of beneficence, it appears to me that the duty of nonmaleficence is recognized as a distinct one, and as *prima facie* more binding. We should not in general consider it justifiable to kill one person in order to keep another alive, or to steal from one in order to give alms to another.

The essential defect of the "ideal utilitarian" theory is that it ignores, or at least does not do full justice to, the highly personal character of duty. If the only duty is to produce the maximum of good, the question who is to have the good—whether it is myself, or my benefactor, or a person to whom I have made a promise to confer that good on him, or a mere fellow man to whom I stand in no such special relation—should make no difference to my having a duty to produce that good. But we are all in fact sure that it makes a vast difference.

One or two other comments must be made on this provisional list of the divisions of duty. (1) The nomenclature is not strictly correct. For by "fidelity" or "gratitude" we mean, strictly, certain states of motivation; and, as I have urged, it is not our duty to have certain motives, but to do certain acts: By "fidelity," for instance, is meant, strictly, the disposition to fulfil promises and implicit promises *because we have made them.* We have no general word to cover the actual fulfilment of promises and implicit promises *irrespective of motive;* and I use "fidelity," loosely but perhaps conveniently, to fill this gap. So too I use "gratitude" for the returning of services, irrespective of motive. The term "justice" is not so much confined, in ordinary usage, to a certain state of motivation, for we should often talk of a man as acting justly even when we did not think his motive was the wish to do what was just simply for the sake of doing so. Less apology is therefore needed for our use of "justice" in this sense. And I have used the word "beneficence" rather than "benevolence," in order to emphasize the fact that it is our duty to do certain things, and not to do them from certain motives.

(2) If the objection be made, that this catalogue of the main types of duty is an unsystematic one resting on no logical principle, it may be replied, first, that it makes no claim to being ultimate. It is a *prima facie* classification of the duties which reflection on our moral convictions seems actually to reveal. And if these convictions are, as I would claim that they are, of the nature of knowledge, and if I have not misstated them, the list will be a list of authentic conditional duties, correct as far as it goes though not necessarily complete. The list of *goods* put forward by the rival theory is reached by exactly the same method—the only sound one in the circumstances—namely, that of direct reflection on what we really think. Loyalty to the facts is worth more than a symmetrical architectonic or a hastily reached simplicity. If further reflection discovers a perfect logical basis for this or for a better classification, so much the better.

(3) It may, again, be objected that our theory that there are these various and often conflicting types of *prima facie* duty leaves us with no principle upon which to discern what is our actual duty in particular circumstances. But this objection is not one which the rival theory is in a position to bring forward. For when we have to choose between the production of two heterogeneous goods, say knowledge and pleasure, the "ideal utilitarian" theory can only fall back on an opinion, for which no logical basis can be offered, that one of the goods is the greater; and this is no better than a similar opinion that one of two duties is the more urgent. And again, when we consider the infinite variety of the effects of our actions in the way of pleasure, it must surely be admitted that the claim which *hedonism* sometimes makes, that it offers a readily applicable criterion of right conduct, is quite illusory.

I am unwilling, however, to content myself with an *argumentum ad hominem*, and I would contend that in principle there is no reason to anticipate that every act that is our duty is so for one and the same reason. Why should two sets of circumstances, or one set of circumstances, *not* possess different characteristics, any one of which makes a certain act our *prima facie* duty? When I ask what it is that makes me in certain cases sure that I have a *prima facie* duty to do so and so, I find that it lies in the fact that I have made a promise; when I ask the same question in another case, I find the answer lies in the fact that I have done a wrong. And if on reflection I find (as I think I do) that neither of these reasons is reducible to the other, I must not on any *a priori* ground assume that such a reduction is possible.

An attempt may be made to arrange in a more systematic way the main types of duty which we have indicated. In the first place it seems self-evident that if there are things that are intrinsically good, it is *prima facie* a duty to bring them into existence rather than not to do so, and to bring as much of them into existence as possible. It will be argued in our fifth chapter that there are three main things that are intrinsically good—virtue, knowledge, and, with certain limitations, pleasure. And since a given virtuous disposition, for instance, is equally good whether it is realized in myself or in another, it seems to be my duty to bring it into existence whether in myself or in another. So too with a given piece of knowledge.

The case of pleasure is difficult; for while we clearly recognize a duty to produce pleasure for others, it is by no means so clear that we recognize a duty to produce pleasure for ourselves. This appears to arise from the following facts. The thought of an act as our duty is one that presupposes a certain amount of reflection about the act; and for that reason does not normally arise in connexion with acts towards which we are already impelled by another strong impulse. So far, the cause of our not thinking of the promotion of our own pleasure as a duty is analogous to the cause which usually prevents a highly sympathetic person from thinking of the promotion of the pleasure of others as a duty. He is impelled so strongly by direct interest in the well-being of others towards promoting their pleasure that he does not stop to ask whether it is his duty to promote it; and we are all impelled so strongly towards the promotion of our own pleasure that we do not stop to ask whether it is a duty or not. But there is a further reason why even when we stop to think about the matter it does not usually present itself as a duty: namely that, since the performance of most of our duties involves the giving up of some pleasure that we desire, the doing of duty and the getting of pleasure for ourselves come by a natural association of ideas to be thought of as incompatible things. This association of ideas is in the main salutary in its operation, since it puts a check on what but for it would be much too strong, the tendency to pursue one's own pleasure without thought of other considerations. Yet if pleasure is good, it seems in the long run clear that it is right to get it for ourselves as well as to produce it for others, when this does not involve the failure to discharge some more stringent *prima facie* duty. The question is a very difficult one, but it seems that this conclusion can be denied only on one or other of three grounds: (1) that pleasure is not *prima facie* good (*i.e.* good when it is neither the actualization of a bad disposition nor undeserved), (2) that there is no *prima facie* duty to produce as much that is good as we can, or (3) that though there is a *prima facie* duty to produce other things that are good, there is no *prima facie* duty to produce pleasure which will be enjoyed by ourselves. I give reasons later for not accepting the first contention. The second hardly admits of argument but seems to me plainly false. The third seems plausible only if we hold that an act that is pleasant or brings pleasure to ourselves must for that reason not be a duty; and this would lead to paradoxical consequences, such as that if a man enjoys giving pleasure to others or working for their moral improvement, it cannot be his duty to do so. Yet it seems to be a very stubborn fact, that in our ordinary consciousness we are not aware of a duty to get pleasure for ourselves; and by way of partial explanation of this I may add that though, as I think, one's own pleasure is a good and there is a duty to produce it, it is only if we *think* of our own pleasure not as simply our own pleasure, but as an objective good, something that an impartial spectator would approve, that we can think of the getting it as a duty; and we do not habitually think of it in this way.

If these contentions are right, what we have called the duty of beneficence and the duty of self-improvement rest on the same ground. No different principles of duty are involved in the two cases.

If we feel a special responsibility for improving our own character rather than that of others, it is not because a special principle is involved, but because we are aware that the one is more under our control than the other. It was on this ground that Kant expressed the practical law of duty in the form "seek to make yourself good and other people happy." He was so persuaded of the internality of virtue that he regarded any attempt by one person to produce virtue in another as bound to produce, at most, only a counterfeit of virtue, the doing of externally right acts not from the true principle of virtuous action but out of regard to another person. It must be admitted that one man cannot compel another to be virtuous; compulsory virtue would just not be virtue. But experience clearly shows that Kant overshoots the mark when he contends that one man cannot do anything to *promote* virtue in another, to bring such influences to bear upon him that his own response to them is more likely to be virtuous than his response to other influences would have been. And our duty to do this is not different in kind from our duty to improve our own characters.

It is equally clear, and clear at an earlier stage of moral development, that if there are things that are bad in themselves we ought, *prima facie*, not to bring them upon others; and on this fact rests the duty of nonmaleficence.

The duty of justice is particularly complicated, and the word is used to cover things which are really very different—things such as the payment of debts, the reparation of injuries done by oneself to another, and the bringing about of a distribution of happiness between other people in proportion to merit. I use the word to denote only the last of these three. In the fifth chapter I shall try to show that besides the three (comparatively) simple goods, virtue, knowledge, and pleasure, there is a more complex good, not reducible to these, consisting in the proportionment of happiness to virtue. The bringing of this about is a duty which we owe to all men alike, though it may be reinforced by special responsibilities that we have undertaken to particular men. This, therefore, with beneficence and self-improvement, comes under the general principle that we should produce as much good as possible, though the good here involved is different in kind from any other.

But besides this general obligation, there are special obligations.

These may arise, in the first place, incidentally, from acts which were not essentially meant to create such an obligation, but which nevertheless create it. From the nature of the case such acts may be of two kinds—the infliction of injuries on others, and the acceptance of benefits from them. It seems clear that these put us under a special obligation to other men, and that only these acts can do so incidentally. From these arise the twin duties of reparation and gratitude.

And finally there are special obligations arising from acts the very intention of which, when they were done, was to put us under such an obligation. The name for such acts is "promises"; the name is wide enough if we are willing to include under it implicit promises, that is, modes of behavior in which without explicit verbal promise we intentionally create an expectation that we can be counted on to behave in a certain way in the interest of another person.

There seem to be, in principle, all the ways in which *prima facie* duties arise. In actual experience they are compounded together in highly complex ways. Thus, for example, the duty of obeying the laws of one's country arises partly (as Socrates contends in the *Crito*) from the duty of gratitude for the benefits one has received from it; partly from the implicit promise to obey which seems to be involved in permanent residence in a country whose laws we know we are *expected* to obey, and still more clearly involved when we ourselves invoke the protection of its laws (this is the truth underlying the doctrine of the social contract); and partly (if we are fortunate in our country) from the fact that its laws are potent instruments for the general good.

Or again, the sense of a general obligation to bring about (so far as we can) a just apportionment of happiness to merit is often greatly reinforced by the fact that many of the existing injustices are due to a social and economic system which we have, not indeed created, but taken part in and assented to; the duty of justice is then reinforced by the duty of reparation.

It is necessary to say something by way of clearing up the relation between *prima facie* duties and the actual or absolute duty to do one particular act in particular circumstances. If, as almost all moralists except Kant are agreed, and as most plain men think, it is sometimes right to tell a lie or to break a promise, it must be maintained that there is a difference between *prima facie* duty and actual or absolute duty. When we think ourselves justified in breaking, and indeed morally obliged to break, a promise in order to relieve someone's distress, we do not for a moment cease to recognize a *prima facie* duty to keep our promise, and this leads us to feel, not indeed shame or repentance, but certainly compunction, for behaving as we do; we recognize, further, that it is our duty to make up somehow to the promisee for the breaking of the promise. We have to distinguish from the characteristic of being our duty that of tending to be our duty. Any act that we do contains various elements in virtue of which it falls under various categories. In virtue of being the breaking of a promise, for instance, it tends to be wrong; in virtue of being an instance of relieving distress it tends to be right. Tendency to be one's duty may be called a parti-resultant attribute, that is, one which belongs to an act in virtue of some one component in its nature. *Being* one's duty is a toti-resultant attribute, one which belongs to an act in virtue of its whole nature and of nothing less than this.[6] This distinction between parti-resultant and toti-resultant attributes is one which we shall meet in another context also.

Another instance of the same distinction may be found in the operation of natural laws. *Qua* subject to the force of gravitation towards some other body, each body tends to move in a particular direction with a particular velocity; but its actual movement depends on *all* the forces to which it is subject. It is only by recognizing this distinction that we can preserve the absoluteness of laws of nature, and only by recognizing a corresponding distinction that we can preserve the absoluteness of the general principles of morality. But an important difference between the two cases must be pointed out. When we say that in virtue of gravitation a body tends to move in a certain way, we are referring to a causal influence actually exercised on it by another body or other bodies. When we say that in virtue of being deliberately untrue a certain remark tends to be wrong, we are referring to no causal relation, to no relation that involves succession in time, but to such a relation as connects the various attributes of a mathematical figure. And if the word "tendency" is thought to suggest too much a causal relation,

---

[6] But cf. the qualification in p. 80, n. 7.

it is better to talk of certain types of act as being *prima facie* right or wrong (or of different persons as having different and possibly conflicting claims upon us), than of their tending to be right or wrong.

Something should be said of the relation between our apprehension of the *prima facie* rightness of certain types of act and our mental attitude towards particular acts. It is proper to use the word "apprehension" in the former case and not in the latter. That an act, *qua* fulfilling a promise, or *qua* effecting a just distribution of good, or *qua* returning services rendered, or *qua* promoting the good of others, or *qua* promoting the virtue or insight of the agent, is *prima facie* right, is self-evident; not in the sense that it is evident from the beginning of our lives, or as soon as we attend to the proposition for the first time, but in the sense that when we have reached sufficient mental maturity and have given sufficient attention to the proposition it is evident without any need of proof, or of evidence beyond itself. It is self-evident just as a mathematical axiom, or the validity of a form of inference, is evident. The moral order expressed in these propositions is just as much part of the fundamental nature of the universe (and, we may add, of any possible universe in which there were moral agents at all) as is the spatial or numerical structure expressed in the axioms of geometry or arithmetic. In our confidence that these propositions are true there is involved the same trust in our reason that is involved in our confidence in mathematics; and we should have no justification for trusting it in the latter sphere and distrusting it in the former. In both cases we are dealing with propositions that cannot be proved, but that just as certainly need no proof.

Some of these general principles of *prima facie* duty may appear to be open to criticism. It may be thought, for example, that the principle of returning good for good is a falling off from the Christian principle, generally and rightly recognized as expressing the highest morality, of returning good for evil. To this it may be replied that I do not suggest that there is a principle commanding us to return good for good and forbidding us to return good for evil, and that I do suggest that there is a positive duty to seek the good of all men. What I maintain is that an act in which good is returned for good is recognized as *specially* binding on us just because it is of that character, and that *ceteris paribus* any one would think it his duty to help his benefactors rather than his enemies, if he could not do both; just as it is generally recognized that *ceteris paribus* we should pay our debts rather than give our money in charity, when we cannot do both. A benefactor is not only a man, calling for our effort on his behalf on that ground, but also our benefactor, calling for our *special* effort on *that* ground.

Our judgements about our actual duty in concrete situations have none of the certainty that attaches to our recognition of the general principles of duty. A statement is certain, that is, is an expression of knowledge, only in one or other of two cases: when it is either self-evident, or a valid conclusion from self-evident premises. And our judgements about our particular duties have neither of these characters. (1) They are not self-evident. Where a possible act is seen to have two characteristics, in virtue of one of which it is *prima facie* right, and in virtue of the other *prima facie* wrong, we are (I think) well aware that we are not certain whether we ought or ought not to do it; that whether we do it or not, we are taking a moral risk. We come in the long run, after consideration, to think one duty more pressing than the other, but we do not feel certain that it is so. And though we do not always recognize that a possible act has two such characteristics, and though there *may* be cases in which it has not, we are never certain that any particular possible act has not, and therefore never certain that it is right, nor certain that it is wrong. For, to go no further in the analysis, it is enough to point out that any particular act will in all probability in the course of time contribute to the bringing about of good or of evil for many human beings, and thus have a *prima facie* rightness or wrongness of which we know nothing. (2) Again, our judgements about our particular duties are not logical conclusions from self-evident premisses. The only possible premises would be the general principles stating their *prima facie* rightness or wrongness *qua* having the different characteristics they do have; and even if we could (as we cannot) apprehend the extent to which an act will tend on the one hand, for example, to bring about advantages for our benefactors, and on the other hand to bring about disadvantages for fellow men who are not our benefactors, there is no principle by which we can draw the conclusion that it is on the whole right or on the whole

wrong. In this respect the judgement as to the rightness of a particular act is just like the judgement as to the beauty of a particular
natural object of work of art. A poem is, for instance, in respect of
certain qualities beautiful and in respect of certain others not beautiful; and our judgement as to the degree of beauty it possesses on the
whole is never reached by logical reasoning from the apprehension
of its particular beauties or particular defects. Both in this and in
the moral case we have more or less probable opinions which are
not logically justified conclusions from the general principles that
are recognized as self-evident.

There is therefore much truth in the description of the right act
as a fortunate act. If we cannot be certain that it is right, it is our
good fortune if the act we do is the right act. This consideration
does not, however, make the doing of our duty a mere matter of
chance. There is a parallel here between the doing of duty and the
doing of what will be to our personal advantage. We never *know*
what act will in the long run be to our advantage. Yet it is certain
that we are more likely in general to secure our advantage if we
estimate to the best of our ability the probable tendencies of our
actions in this respect, than if we act on caprice. And similarly we
are more likely to do our duty if we reflect to the best of our
ability on the *prima facie* rightness or wrongness of various possible
acts in virtue of the characteristics we perceive them to have, than
if we act without reflection. With this greater likelihood we must be
content.

Many people would be inclined to say that the right act for me
is not that whose general nature I have been describing, namely,
that which if I were omniscient I should see to be my duty, but that
which on all the evidence available to me I should think to be my
duty. But suppose that from the state of partial knowledge in
which I think act *A* to be my duty, I could pass to a state of perfect knowledge in which I saw act *B* to be my duty, should I not
say "act *B* was the right act for me to do"? I should no doubt add
"though I am not to be blamed for doing act *A*." But in adding
this, am I not passing from the question "what is right" to the question "what is morally good"? At the same time I am not making the
full passage from the one notion to the other; for in order that the

act should be morally good, or an act I am not to be blamed for doing, it must not merely be the act which it is reasonable for me to think my duty; it must also be done for that reason, or from some other morally good motive. Thus the conception of the right act as the act which it is reasonable for me to think my duty is an unsatisfactory compromise between the true notion of the right act and the notion of the morally good action.

The general principles of duty are obviously not self-evident from the beginning of our lives. How do they come to be so? The answer is, that they come to be self-evident to us just as mathematical axioms do. We find by experience that this couple of matches and that couple make four matches, that this couple of balls on a wire and that couple make four balls: and by reflection on these and similar discoveries we come to see that it is of the nature of two and two to make four. In a precisely similar way, we see the *prima facie* rightness of an act which would be the fulfilment of a particular promise, and of another which would be the fulfilment of another promise, and when we have reached sufficient maturity to think in general terms, we apprehend *prima facie* rightness to belong to the nature of any fulfilment of promise. What comes first in time is the apprehension of the self-evident *prima facie* rightness of an individual act of a particular type. From this we come by reflection to apprehend the self-evident general principle of *prima facie* duty. From this, too, perhaps along with the apprehension of the self-evident *prima facie* rightness of the same act in virtue of its having another characteristic as well, and perhaps in spite of the apprehension of its *prima facie* wrongness in virtue of its having some third characteristic, we come to believe something not self-evident at all, but an object of probable opinion, namely, that this particular act is (not *prima facie* but) actually right.

In this respect there is an important difference between rightness and mathematical properties. A triangle which is isosceles necessarily has two of its angles equal, whatever other characteristics the triangle may have—whatever, for instance, be its area, or the size of its third angle. The equality of the two angles is a parti-resultant attribute. And the same is true of all mathematical attributes. It is true, I may add, of *prima facie* rightness. But no act is ever, in virtue of falling under some general description, necessarily actually right; its rightness depends on its whole nature[7] and not on any element in it. The reason is that no mathematical object (no figure, for instance, or angle) ever has two characteristics that tend to give it opposite resultant characteristics, while moral acts often (as every one knows) and indeed always (as on reflection we must admit) have different characteristics that tend to make them at the same time *prima facie* right and *prima facie* wrong; there is probably no act, for instance, which does good to any one without doing harm to some one else and *vice versa*.

Supposing it to be agreed, as on reflection it must, that no one *means* by "right" just productive of the best possible consequences, or "optimific," the attributes "right" and "optimific" might stand in either of two kinds of relation to each other. (1) They might be so related that we could apprehend *a priori*, either immediately or deductively, that any act that is optimific is right and any act that is right is optimific, as we can apprehend that any triangle that is equilateral is equiangular and *vice versa*. Professor Moore's position is, I think, that the coextensiveness of "right" and "optimific" is apprehended immediately.[8] He rejects the possibility of any proof of it. Or (2) the two attributes might be such that the question whether they are invariably connected had been answered by means of an inductive inquiry. Now at first glance it might seem as if the constant connexion of the two attributes could be immediately apprehended. It might seem absurd to suggest that it could be right for any one to do an act which would produce consequences less good than those which would be produced by some other act in his power. Yet a little thought will convince us that this is not absurd. The type of case in which it is easiest to see that this is so is, perhaps, that in which one has made a promise. In such a case we all think that *prima facie* it is our duty to fulfil the promise irrespective of the precise goodness of the total consequences. And though we do not think it is

[7] To avoid complicating unduly the statement of the general view I am putting forward, I have here rather overstated it. Any act is the origination of a great variety of things many of which make no difference to its rightness or wrongness. But there are always many elements in its nature (*i.e.* in what it is the origination of) that make a difference to its rightness or wrongness, and no element in its nature can be dismissed without consideration as indifferent.

[8] *Ethics*, 181.

necessarily our actual or absolute duty to do so, we are far from thinking that any, even the slightest, gain in the value of the total consequences will necessarily justify us in doing something else instead. Suppose, to simplify the case by abstraction, that the fulfilment of a promise to . . . would produce 1,000 units of good [9] for him, but that by doing some other act I could produce 1,001 units of good for *B*, by whom I have made no promise, the other consequences of the two acts being of equal value; should we really think it self-evident that it was our duty to do the second act and not the first? I think not. We should, I fancy, hold that only a much greater disparity of value between the total consequences would justify us in failing to discharge our *prima facie* duty to *A*. After all, a promise is a promise, and is not to be treated so lightly as the theory we are examining would imply. What, exactly, a promise is, is not so easy to determine, but we are surely agreed that it constitutes a serious moral limitation to our freedom of action. To produce the 1,001 units of good for *B* rather than fulfil our promise to *A* would be to take, not perhaps our duty as philanthropists too seriously, but certainly our duty as makers of promises too lightly.

Or consider another phase of the same problem. If I have promised to confer on *A* a particular benefit containing 1,000 units of good, it is self-evident that if by doing some different act I could produce 1,001 units of good for *A* himself (the other consequences of the two acts being supposed equal in value), it would be right for me to do so? Again, I think not. Apart from my general *prima facie* duty to do *A* what good I can, I have another *prima facie* duty to do him the particular service I have promised to do him, and this is not to be set aside in consequence of a disparity of good of the order of 1,001 to 1,000, though a much greater disparity might justify me in so doing.

Or again, suppose that *A* is a very good and *B* a very bad man, should I then, even when I have made no promise, think it self-evidently right to produce 1,001 units of good for *B* rather than 1,000 for *A*? Surely not. I should be sensible of a *prima facie* duty of

[9] I am assuming that good is objectively quantitative, but not that we can accurately assign an exact quantitative measure to it. Since it is of a definite amount, we can make the *supposition* that its amount is so-and-so, though we cannot with any confidence *assert* that it is.

justice, that is, of producing a distribution of goods in proportion to merit, which is not outweighed by such a slight disparity in the total goods to be produced.

Such instances—and they might easily be added to—make it clear that there is no self-evident connexion between the attributes "right" and "optimific." The theory we are examining has a certain attractiveness when applied to our decision that a particular act is our duty (though I have tried to show that it does not agree with our actual moral judgements even here). But it is not even plausible when applied to our recognition of *prima facie* duty. For if it were self-evident that the right coincides with the optimific, it should be self-evident that what is *prima facie* right is *prima facie* optimific. But whereas we are certain that keeping a promise is *prima facie* right, we are not certain that it is *prima facie* optimific (though we are perhaps certain that it is *prima facie* bonific). Our certainty that it is *prima facie* right depends not on its consequences but on its being the fulfilment of a promise. The theory we are examining involves too much difference between the evident ground of our conviction about *prima facie* duty and the alleged ground of our conviction about actual duty.

The coextensiveness of the right and the optimific is, then, not self-evident. And I can see no way of proving it deductively; nor, so far as I know, has anyone tried to do so. There remains the question whether it can be established inductively. Such an inquiry, to be conclusive, would have to be very thorough and extensive. We should have to take a large variety of the acts which we, to the best of our ability, judge to be right. We should have to trace as far as possible their consequences, not only for the persons directly affected but also for those indirectly affected, and to these no limit can be set. To make our inquiry thoroughly conclusive, we should have to do what we cannot do, namely, trace these consequences into an unending future. And even to make it reasonably conclusive, we should have to trace them far into the future. It is clear that the most we could possibly say is that a large variety of typical acts that are judged right appear, so far as we can trace their consequences, to produce more good than any other acts possible to the agents in the circumstances. And such a result falls far short of proving the constant connexion of the two attributes. But it is surely clear that no inductive inquiry justifying even this result has ever been carried through. The advocates of utilitarian systems have been so much persuaded either of the identity or of the self-evident connexion of the attributes "right" and "optimific" (or "felicific") that they have not attempted even such an inductive inquiry as is possible. And in view of the enormous complexity of the task and the inevitable inconclusiveness of the result, it is worth no one's while to make the attempt. What, after all, would be gained by it? If, as I have tried to show, for an act to be right and to be optimific are not the same thing, and an act's being optimific is not even the ground of its being right, then if we could ask ourselves (though the question is really unmeaning) which we ought to do, right acts because they are right or optimific acts because they are optimific, our answer must be "the former." If they are optimific as well as right, that is interesting but not morally important; if not, we still ought to do them (which is only another way of saying that they *are* the right acts), and the question whether they are optimific has no importance for moral theory.

There is one direction in which a fairly serious attempt has been made to show the connexion of the attributes "right" and "optimific." One of the most evident facts of our moral consciousness is the sense which we have of the sanctity of promises, a sense which does not, on the face of it, involve the thought that one will be bringing more good into existence by fulfilling the promise than by breaking it. It is plain, I think, that in our normal thought we consider that the fact that we have made a promise is in itself sufficient to create a duty of keeping it, the sense of duty resting on remembrance of the past promise and not on thoughts of the future consequences of its fulfilment. Utilitarianism tries to show that this is not so, that the sanctity of promises rests on the good consequences of the fulfilment of them and the bad consequences of their nonfulfilment. It does so in this way: it points out that when you break a promise you not only fail to confer a certain advantage on your promise but you diminish his confidence, and indirectly the confidence of others, in the fulfilment of promises. You thus strike a blow at one of the devices that have been found most useful in the relations between man and man—the device on which, for example, the whole system of commercial credit rests—and you tend to bring about a state of things wherein each man, being entirely unable to rely on the keeping of promises by others, will have to do everything for himself, to the enormous impoverishment of human well-being.

To put the matter otherwise, utilitarians say that when a promise ought to be kept it is because the total good to be produced by keeping it is greater than the total good to be produced by breaking it, the former including as its main element the maintenance and strengthening of general mutual confidence, and the latter being greatly diminished by a weakening of this confidence. They say, in fact, that the case I put some pages back[10] never arises—the case in which by fulfilling a promise I shall bring into being 1,000 units of good for my promisee, and by breaking it 1,001 units of good for some one else, the other effects of the two acts being of equal value. The other effects, they say, never are of equal value. By keeping my promise I am helping to strengthen the system of mutual confidence; by breaking it I am helping to weaken this; so that really the first act produces $1,000 + x$ units of good, and the second $1,001 - y$ units, and the difference between $+x$ and $-y$ is enough to outweigh the slight superiority in the *immediate* effects of the second act. In answer to this it may be pointed out that there must be *some* amount of good that exceeds the difference between $+x$ and $-y$ (*i.e.* exceeds $x + y$); say, $x + y + z$. Let us suppose the *immediate* good effects of the second act to be assessed not at 1,001 but at $1,000 + x + y + z$. Then its *net* good effects are $1,000 + x + z$, that is, greater than those of the fulfilment of the promise; and the utilitarian is bound to say forthwith that the promise should be broken. Now, we may ask whether that is really the way we think about promises? Do we really think that the production of the slightest balance of good, no matter who will enjoy it, by the breach of a promise frees us from the obligation to keep our promise? We need not doubt that a system by which promises are made and kept is one that has great advantages for the general well-being. But that is not the whole truth. To make a promise is not merely to adapt an ingenious device for promoting the general well-being; it is to put oneself in a new relation to one person in particular, a relation

[10] P. 81.

which creates a specifically new *prima facie* duty to him, not reducible to the duty of promoting the general well-being of society. By all means let us try to foresee the net good effects of keeping one's promise and the net good effects of breaking it, but even if we assess the first at $1,000 + x$ and the second at $1,000 + x + z$, the question still remains whether it is not our duty to fulfil the promise. It may be suspected, too, that the effect of a single keeping or breaking of a promise in strengthening or weakening the fabric of mutual confidence is greatly exaggerated by the theory we are examining. And if we suppose two men dying together alone, do we think that the duty of one to fulfil before he dies a promise he has made to the other would be extinguished by the fact that neither act would have any effect on the general confidence? Any one who holds this may be suspected of not having reflected on what a promise is.

I conclude that the attributes "right" and "optimific" are not identical, and that we do not know either by intuition, by deduction, or by induction that they coincide in their application, still less that the latter is the foundation of the former. It must be added, however, that if we are ever under no special obligation such as that of fidelity to a promisee or of gratitude to a benefactor, we ought to do what will produce most good; and that even when we are under a special obligation the tendency of acts to promote general good is one of the main factors in determining whether they are right.

In what has preceded, a good deal of use has been made of "what we really think" about moral questions; a certain theory has been rejected because it does not agree with what we really think. It might be said that this is in principle wrong; that we should not be content to expound what our present moral consciousness tells us but should aim at a criticism of our existing moral consciousness in the light of theory. Now I do not doubt that the moral consciousness of men has in detail undergone a good deal of modification as regards the things we think right, at the hands of moral theory. But if we are told, for instance, that we should give up our view that there is a special obligatoriness attaching to the keeping of promises because it is self-evident that the only duty is to produce as much good as possible, we have to ask ourselves whether we really, when we reflect, *are* convinced that this is self-evident, and whether we really *can* get rid of our view that promise-keeping has a bindingness independent of productiveness of maximum good. In my own experience I find that I cannot, in spite of a very genuine attempt to do so; and I venture to think that most people will find the same, and that just because they cannot lose the sense of special obligation, they cannot accept as self-evident, or even as true, the theory which would require them to do so. In fact it seems, on reflection, self-evident that a promise, simply as such, is something that *prima facie* ought to be kept, and it does *not,* on reflection, seem self-evident that production of maximum good is the only thing that makes an act obligatory. And to ask us to give up at the bidding of a theory our actual apprehension of what is right and what is wrong seems like asking people to repudiate their actual experience of beauty, at the bidding of a theory which says "only that which satisfies such and such conditions can be beautiful." If what I have called our actual apprehension is (as I would maintain that it is) truly an apprehension, that is, an instance of knowledge, the request is nothing less than absurd.

I would maintain, in fact, that what we are apt to describe as "what we think" about moral questions contains a considerable amount that we do not think but know, and that this forms the standard by reference to which the truth of any moral theory has to be tested, instead of having itself to be tested by reference to any theory. I hope that I have in what precedes indicated what in my view these elements of knowledge are that are involved in our ordinary moral consciousness.

It would be a mistake to found a natural science on "what we really think," that is, on what reasonably thoughtful and well-educated people think about the subjects of the science before they have studied them scientifically. For such opinions are interpretations, and often misinterpretations, of sense-experience; and the man of science must appeal from these to sense-experience itself, which furnishes his real data. In ethics no such appeal is possible. We have no more direct way of access to the facts about rightness and goodness and about what things are right or good, than by thinking about them; the moral convictions of thoughtful and well-educated people are the data of ethics just as sense-perceptions are the data of a natural science. Just as some of the latter have to be rejected as illusory, so have some of the former; but as the latter are rejected only when they are in conflict with other more accurate sense-perceptions, the former are rejected only when they are in conflict with other convictions which stand better the test of reflection. The existing body of moral convictions of the best people is the cumulative product of the moral reflection of many generations, which has developed an extremely delicate power of appreciation of moral distinctions; and this the theorist cannot afford to treat with anything other than the greatest respect. The verdicts of the moral consciousness of the best people are the foundation on which he must build; though he must first compare them with one another and eliminate any contradictions they may contain.

It is worth while to try to state more definitely the nature of the acts that are right. We may try to state first what (if anything) is the universal nature of *all* acts that are right. It is obvious that any of the acts that we do has countless effects, directly or indirectly, on countless people, and the probability is that any act, however right it be, will have adverse effects (though these may be very trivial) on some innocent people. Similarly, any wrong act will probably have beneficial effects on some deserving people. Every act therefore, viewed in some aspects, will be *prima facie* right, and viewed in others, *prima facie* wrong, and right acts can be distinguished from wrong acts only as being those which, of all those possible for the agent in the circumstances, have the greatest balance of *prima facie* rightness, in those respects in which they are *prima facie* right, over their *prima facie* wrongness, in those respects in which they are *prima facie* wrong—*prima facie* rightness and wrongness being understood in the sense previously explained. For the estimation of the comparative stringency of these *prima facie* obligations no general rules can, so far as I can see, be laid down. We can only say that a great deal of stringency belongs to the duties of "perfect obligation"—the duties of keeping our promises, of repairing wrongs we have done, and of returning the equivalent of services we have received. For the rest, ἐν τῇ αἰσθήσει ἡ κρίσις.[11] This sense of our par-

[11] "The decision rests with perception." Aristotle, *Nicomachean Ethics.* 1109 b 23, 1126 b 4.

ticular duty in particular circumstances, preceded and informed by
the fullest reflection we can bestow on the act in all its bearings,
is highly fallible, but it is the only guide we have to our duty.

When we turn to consider the nature of individual right acts,
the first point to which attention should be called is that any act
may be correctly described in an indefinite, and in principle infinite, number of ways. An act is the production of a change in the
state of affairs (if we ignore, for simplicity's sake, the comparatively
few cases in which it is the maintenance of an existing state of affairs;
cases which, I think, raise no special difficulty). Now the only
changes we can *directly* produce are changes in our own bodies or
in our own minds. But these are not, as such, what as a rule we
think it our duty to produce. Consider some comparatively simple
act, such as telling the truth or fulfilling a promise. In the first case
what I produce directly is movements of my vocal organs. But
what I think it my duty to produce is a true view in some one else's
mind about some fact, and between my movement of my vocal organs and this result there intervenes a series of physical events and
events in his mind. Again, in the second case, I may have promised,
for instance, to return a book to a friend. I may be able, by a series
of movements of my legs and hands, to place it in his hands. But
what I am just as likely to do, and to think I have done my duty
in doing, is to send it by a messenger or to hand it to his servant
or to send it by post; and in each of these cases what I *do* directly
is worthless in itself and is connected by a series of intermediate
links with what I do think it is my duty to bring about, namely, his
receiving what I have promised to return to him. This being so, it
seems as if what I *do* has no obligatoriness in itself and as if one
or other of three accounts should be given of the matter, each of
which makes rightness not belong to what I do, considered in its
own nature.

(1) One of them would be that what is obligatory is not *doing*
anything in the natural sense of producing any change in the state
of affairs, but *aiming at* something—at, for instance, my friend's reception of the book. But this account will not do. For (a) to aim at
something is to act from a motive consisting of the wish to bring
that thing about. But we have seen that motive never forms part of
the content of our duty; if anything is certain about morals, that,

What Makes Right Acts Right? / 89

I think, is certain. And (b) if I have promised to return the book to my friend, I obviously do not fulfil my promise and do my duty merely by aiming at his receiving the book; I must see that he actually receives it. (2) A more plausible account is that which says I must do that which is likely to produce the result. But this account is open to the second of these objections, and probably also to the first. For in the first place, however likely my act may seem, even on careful consideration, and even however likely it may in fact be, to produce the result, if it does not produce it I have not done what I promised to do, that is, have not done my duty. And secondly, when it is said that I ought to do what is likely to produce the result, what is *probably* meant is that I ought to do a certain thing as a result of the wish to produce a certain result, and of the thought that my act is likely to produce it; and this again introduces motive into the content of duty. (3) Much the most plausible of the three accounts is that which says, "I ought to do that which will actually produce a certain result." This escapes objection (b). Whether it escapes objection (a) or not depends on what exactly is meant. If it is meant that I ought to do a certain thing from the wish to produce a certain result and the thought that it will do so, the account is still open to objection (a). But if it is meant simply that I ought to do a certain thing, and that the reason why I ought to do it is that it will produce a certain result, objection (a) is avoided. Now this account in its second form is that which utilitarianism gives. It says what is right is certain acts, not certain acts motivated in a certain way; and it says that acts are never right by their own nature but by virtue of the goodness of their actual results. And this account is, I think, clearly nearer the truth than one which makes the rightness of an act depend on the goodness of either the *intended* or the *likely* results.

Nevertheless, this account appears not to be the true one. For it implies that what we consider right or our duty is what we do *directly*. It is this, for example, the packing up and posting of the book, that derives its moral significance not from its own nature but from its consequences. But this is *not* what we should describe, strictly, as our duty; our duty is to fulfil our promise, that is, to put the book into our friend's possession. This we consider obligatory in its own nature, just because it is a fulfilment of promise, and not because of *its* consequences. But, it might be replied by the utilitarian, I do not do this; I only do something that leads up to this, and what I do has no moral significance in itself but only because of its consequences. In answer to this, however, we may point out that a cause produces not only its immediate, but also its remote consequences, and the latter no less than the former. I, therefore, not only produce the immediate movements of parts of my body but also my friend's reception of the book, which results from these. Or, if this be objected to on the grounds that I can hardly be said to have produced my friend's reception of the book when I have packed and posted it, owing to the time that has still to elapse before he receives it, and that to say I have produced the result hardly does justice to the part played by the Post Office, we may at least say that I have *secured* my friend's reception of the book. What I do is as truly describable in this way as by saying that it is the packing and posting of a book. (It is equally truly describable in many other ways; for example, I have provided a few moments' employment for Post Office officials. But this is irrelevant to the argument.) And if we ask ourselves whether it is *qua* the packing and posting of a book, or *qua* the securing of my friend's getting what I have promised to return to him, that my action is right, it is clear that it is in the second capacity that it is right; and in this capacity, the only capacity in which it is right, it is right by its own nature and not because of its consequences.

This account may no doubt be objected to, on the ground that we are ignoring the freedom of will of the other agents—the sorter and the postman, for instance—who are equally responsible for the result. Society, it may be said, is not like a machine, in which event follows event by rigorous necessity. Some one may, for instance, in the exercise of his freedom of will, steal the book on the way. But it is to be observed that I have excluded that case, and any similar case. I am dealing with the case in which I secure my friend's receiving the book; and if he does not receive it I have not secured his receiving it. If on the other hand the book reaches its destination, that alone shows that, the system of things being what it is, the trains by which the book travels and the railway lines along which it travels being such as they are and subject to the laws they are subject to, the postal officials who handle it being such as they are, having the motives they have and being subject to the psychological laws they are subject to, my posting the book was the one further thing which was sufficient to procure my friend's receiving it. If it had not been sufficient, the result would not have followed. The attainment of the result proves the sufficiency of the means. The objection in fact rests on the supposition that there can be unmotived action, that is, an event without a cause, and may be refuted by reflection on the universality of the law of causation.

It is equally true that nonattainment of the result proves the insufficiency of the means. If the book had been destroyed in a railway accident or stolen by a dishonest postman, that would prove that my immediate act was not sufficient to produce the desired result. We get the curious consequence that however carelessly I pack or dispatch the book, if it comes to hand I have done my duty, and however carefully I have acted, if the book does not come to hand I have not done my duty. Success and failure are the only test, and a sufficient test, of the performance of duty. Of course, I should deserve more praise in the second case than in the first; but that is an entirely different question; we must not mix up the question of right and wrong with that of the morally good and the morally bad. And that our conclusion is not as strange as at first sight it might seem is shown by the fact that if the carelessly dispatched book comes to hand, it is not my duty to send another copy, while if the carefully dispatched book does not come to hand I must send another copy to replace it. In the first case I have not my duty still to do, which shows that I have done it; in the second I have it still to do, which shows that I have not done it.

We have reached the result that my act is right *qua* being an ensuring of one of the particular states of affairs of which it is an ensuring, namely, in the case we have taken, of my friend's receiving the book I have promised to return to him. But this answer requires some correction; for it refers only to the *prima facie* rightness of my act. If to be a fulfilment of promise were a sufficient ground of the rightness of an act, all fulfilments of promises would be right, whereas it seems clear that there are cases in which some other *prima facie* duty overrides the *prima facie* duty of fulfilling a promise. The more correct answer would be that the ground of the actual rightness of the act is that, of all acts possible for the agent in the circumstances, it is that whose *prima facie* rightness in the respects in which it is *prima facie* right most outweighs its *prima facie* wrongness in any respects in which it is *prima facie* wrong. But since its *prima facie* rightness is mainly due to its being a fulfilment of promise, we may call its being so the salient element in the ground of its rightness.

Subject to this qualification, then, it is as being the production (or if we prefer the word, the securing or ensuring) of the reception by my friend of what I have promised him (or in other words as the fulfilment of my promise) that my act is right. It is not right as a packing and posting of a book. The packing and posting of the book is only incidentally right, right only because it is a fulfilment of promise, which is what is directly or essentially right.

Our duty, then, is not to do certain things which will produce certain results. Our acts, at any rate our acts of special obligation, are not right because they will produce certain results—which is the view common to all forms of utilitarianism. To say that is to say that in the case in question what is essentially right is to pack and post a book, whereas what is essentially right is to secure the possession by my friend of what I have promised to return to him. An act is not right because it, being one thing, produces good results different from itself; it is right because it is itself the production of a certain state of affairs. Such production is right in itself, apart from any consequence.

But, it might be said, this analysis applies only to acts of special obligation; the utilitarian account still holds good for the acts in which we are not under a special obligation to any person or set of persons but only under that of augmenting the general good. Now merely to have established that there *are* special obligations to do certain things irrespective of their consequences would be already to have made a considerable breach in the utilitarian walls; for according to utilitarianism there is no such thing, there is only the single obligation to promote the general good. But, further, on reflection it is clear that just as (in the case we have taken) my act is not only the packing and posting of a book but the fulfilling of a promise, and just as it is in the latter capacity and not in the former that it is my duty, so an act whereby I augment the general good is not only, let us say, the writing of a begging letter on behalf of a hospital, but the producing (or ensuring) of whatever good ensues therefrom, and it is in the latter capacity and not in the former that it is right, if it *is* right. That which is right is right not because it is an act, one thing, which will produce another thing, an increase of the general welfare, but because it is itself the producing of an increase in the general welfare. Or, to qualify this in the necessary way, its being the production of an increase in the general welfare is the salient element in the ground of its rightness. Just as before we were led to recognize the *prima facie* rightness of the fulfilment of promises, we are now led to recognize the *prima facie* rightness of promoting the general welfare. In both cases we have to recognize the *intrinsic* rightness of a certain type of act, not depending on its consequences but on its own nature.

JONATHAN HARRISON

Utilitarianism, Universalisation, and Our Duty to Be Just

> In considering what common interest requires, we are, besides the
> immediate effects of actions, to consider what their general tend-
> encies are, what they open the way to, and what would actually be
> the consequences if all were to act alike. If under the pretence of
> greater indigence, superfluity to the owner, or intention to give to a
> worthier person, I may take away a man's property, or adjudge it
> from him in a court of justice; another or all, in the same circum-
> stances may do so; and thus the boundaries of property would be
> overthrown, and general anarchy, distrust and savageness be intro-
> duced.—Richard Price.[1]

According to Utilitarianism, it is often said, an action is right if
it produces at least as much good as any other action which the
agent could have done in the circumstances in which he was placed.
Besides being right, it is also a duty, if it produces more good than
any other action that the agent could have done. When we are faced
with a situation in which we have to choose between a number of
actions, each of which would produce as much good or more than
anything else we could do, but of none of which is it true that they
would produce more good than anything else we could do, then we

* From *Proceedings of the Aristotelian Society*, 1952–1953, pp. 105–34. Reprinted by the courtesy of the Editor of the Aristotelian Society. Copyright
1952 The Aristotelian Society.

[1] Richard Price: *A Review of the Principal Questions in Morals,* edited by
D. Daiches Raphael, p. 164.

have not a duty to perform any particular one of these actions to the exclusion of the others. What is our duty is to do one or other of these actions; but it is a matter of indifference which of them we do, and we have done our duty, whichever one of them we perform.[2]

There are, therefore, some right actions which are not duties, and so the words "right" and "a duty" cannot mean the same thing. This fact has been regarded as unimportant,[3] because it has been supposed that the circumstances in which we are faced with a choice between a number of right actions, none of which are duties, occur but seldom.

However, it seems to me that such situations, so far from being rare, are arising all the time. At any moment of the day, when I am not engaged in doing anything in particular, there are at least half a dozen actions I can think of which I could do, which it would be perfectly right for me to do, but none of which could, by any stretch of the imagination, be said to be duties. It is often supposed that, in such circumstances, I have no duties, but this is a mistake. Among the actions which I could do at this moment are some wrong ones; I might, for example, throw my muffin in my friend's face, or wantonly break the window of the cafe in which I am drinking tea with him. Since it is within my power to perform, at this very moment, some wrong actions, I must, at this very moment, have some duty incumbent upon me, namely, the duty of refraining from performing any of these wrong actions. And furthermore, a man of more ascetic temperament and sterner moral character than myself might well argue that, at this very moment, I was not doing my duty; that my money might be better employed in succouring the needy; my time in furthering the development of a noble cause; my mind in contemplating the benevolence of my Maker or the enormities of my sins.

For these reasons, it seems to me that, so far from right actions almost always being duties, right actions are hardly ever duties. What is my duty is to perform one of the number of alternative right actions which I could perform; in doing any one of them I

---

[2] See G. E. Moore: *Ethics*, pp. 32–35. The definition of utilitarianism used here would not have satisfied Professor Moore, but it will do for our purposes.
[3] See W. D. Ross: *The Right and the Good*, pp. 3–4.

do my duty, though I could equally well have done it in doing any other. The occasion when we can say of one particular action that it, and it alone, is a duty, occurs comparatively seldom.

Utilitarianism might, then, be defined as the theory which holds that an action is right if there is no action within the power of the agent which would produce more good than it, and that it is my duty to perform some right action or other. The circumstances in which there is only one right action within the power of the agent will fall under this principle as a special case, and, when this special case arises, that right action will also be a duty.

I will not bore my readers by citing any of the well-known objections to utilitarianism, but there is one particular difficulty in this theory which, for the purpose of this article, is of special interest. There are some actions which we think we have a duty to do, although they themselves produce no good consequences, because such actions would produce good consequences if they were generally practised. There are some actions which we think we have a duty to refrain from doing, even though they themselves produce no harmful consequences, because such actions would produce harmful consequences if the performance of them became the general rule. I think I have a duty to vote for that person whose party I think would govern the nation best, although I do not think that the addition of my vote to the total number of votes which are cast for him is going to make any difference to the result of the election, simply because I realise that, if all his other supporters were to do as I do, and fail to go to the polls, the man would not be elected. I refrain from walking on the grass of a well-kept park lawn, not because I think that my walking on the grass is going to damage the lawn to such an extent as to detract from anybody's pleasure in contemplating it, but because I realise that, if everybody else who walked in the park were to do likewise, the grass in the park would be spoilt. These two duties cannot be derived from the duty of setting a good example, or of refraining from setting a bad example, for I should still feel them incumbent upon me, even if no one were to know that I had defaced my ballot paper, and even if the park was empty of everyone but me.

Such facts, if they are facts, have not been entirely neglected by Utilitarians. Hume, for example, may have had them in mind when he distinguished between justice and benevolence. Of the social virtues of benevolence and humanity he says:

> And as the good, resulting from their benign influence is in itself complete and entire, it also excites the moral sentiment of approbation, without any reflection on farther consequences, and without any more enlarged views of the concurrence or imitation of the other members of society.[4]

Whereas of justice he says:

> The case is not the same with the social virtues of justice and fidelity. They are highly useful, or indeed absolutely necessary to the well-being of mankind; but the benefit resulting from them is not the consequence of every individual single act; but arises from the whole scheme or system concurred in by the whole, or the greater part of the society.[5]

Comparing the virtues of justice and benevolence, he says:

> The happiness and prosperity of mankind, arising from the social virtue of benevolence and its subdivisions, may be compared to a wall, built by many hands, which still rises by each stone that is heaped upon it, and receives increase proportional to the diligence and care of each workman. The same happiness, raised by the social virtue of justice and its subdivisions, may be compared to the building of a vault, where each individual stone would, of itself, fall to the ground; nor is the whole fabric supported but by the mutual assistance and combination of its corresponding parts.[6]

Benevolent actions, if I have interpreted Hume rightly, themselves produce good consequences, and would produce good consequences whether anybody else performed benevolent actions or not. A just action, however, would not produce good consequences if it was the only instance of its kind. Just actions only produce good consequences so long as the performance of just actions is the rule rather than the exception. This is why one may often be bound to perform a just action which has consequences which are harmful. I must perform it, even when it itself has harmful consequences, because it is an action of a kind the general performance of which is necessary to society. This is why justice is "conventional" in a way

---

[4] L. A. Selby-Bigge: *Hume's Enquiries*, second edition, 1902, p. 304.
[5] *Loc. cit.*
[6] *Op. cit.*, p. 305.

in which benevolence is not. Justice is conventional in that the benefit to be derived from it depends upon its customary observance. No benefit will be obtained from my practice of justice unless my fellows practise it too, and the same is true of them. This is not to say that I make an explicit agreement with them that we shall all behave justly in order to gain the benefits of justice. Indeed, our obligation to be just could not be derived from any such agreement, because the obligation to keep agreements is itself a subdivision of justice. Both I and my neighbours are not just because we agree to be just, but because we each realise that the common practice of justice is in the interest of all of us.

However, it is not certain that Hume did hold the view which I have just attributed to him. This view may easily be confused with, and Hume himself, I am afraid, failed to distinguish it from, another rather similar view. There are some actions which, besides being of a sort which would produce good consequences if generally performed, are themselves necessary to the production of these good consequences. If two men are rowing a boat, the boat will progress only so long as they both row, and will fail to progress if either of them stop rowing. In this case, the actions of either oarsman are necessary if the good which consists in the progress of the boat is to be secured. Such actions, since they are necessary conditions of the production of a certain good, do themselves produce good consequences, and so they must clearly be distinguished from those actions which, though they are of a sort the general performance of which would produce good consequences, do not produce good consequences themselves. Moreover, the good which consists in the movement of the boat cannot be split into parts, and part attributed to the actions of one oarsman, and part to the actions of the other; the whole of this good must be produced, or none of it. Hence the good in question must be considered as being equally the consequence of the actions of either man, and it is the whole of this good which each man must take into account when he is considering whether or not he has a duty to row. Now it may have been Hume's view that justice is a duty, not because just actions are of a sort which would produce good consequences if generally practised, but because just actions are severally necessary if any good is to be produced by the general practice of justice.

There are arguments which might be used to try to show that Hume held the latter of the two views which I have just distinguished; which tend to show that Hume thought that we had a duty to be just because, if we were not just, the whole of the good consequent upon the general performance of justice would be lost; rather than that he thought that we should perform just actions because they were of a sort the general performance of which would produce good consequences, even when they themselves did not. In the first place, he sometimes speaks as if the performance of every just action is necessary if any just action is to produce good consequences. I must be just, even when it seems that the consequences of my being just are bad, because, if I am not just, the good which the general practice of justice brings about will be lost. In the second place, he thinks that, in a state of nature, it will be nobody's duty to be just, because if, in such a state, only one of us behaves justly, no good will result. Whereas what he should have said—and, perhaps, what he would have said—if he had held that a just action is made right by the fact that it is of a sort the general performance of which would produce good consequences, is, that it is our duty to be just, even in a state of nature. For it is still true, even in a state of nature, that the general performance of just actions would produce good consequences, even though individual just actions, performed in that state, do not produce good consequences; hence, it seems, we would have a duty to be just in a state of nature, even if, by being just, we produce consequences which are indifferent, or even bad.

The fact that Hume thought that we would not have a duty to be just in a state of nature, and the fact that he sometimes speaks as if the performance of every just action is necessary if any just action is to have good consequences, seems to indicate that Hume thought that we had a duty to perform just actions because they, together with other just actions, were severally necessary to the production of the good resultant upon the practice of justice. But there are some arguments which tend to show, either that he thought that we had a duty to practise just actions because they were of a sort the general performance of which would have good consequences, or that, if he did not actually hold this, his theory is as a result a worse one than I have supposed it to be.

Firstly, the view that we must be just in this particular case, so that the good consequent upon the practice of justice as a whole should be brought about, is unrealistic. It is simply false that the performance of every just action is necessary if the good produced by the practice of justice is to be secured. If this were true, the human race would have perished miserably many years ago. An occasional act of injustice here and there does not undermine the whole beneficial effect of the practice of justice, and, if such actions are performed in secret, they may sometimes not even produce any harmful effects at all.

Secondly, the view that we must be just, because just actions are severally necessary to the production of the good of justice, would make our duty to be just more rigid than we in fact believe it to be. Our normal view on the practice of justice in hard cases is this. We think that we should not turn aside from justice whenever it seems that an unjust action would produce some good, but, on the other hand, we do think that there are occasions on which unjust actions should be performed, because the good to be gained is considerable. But, if the whole of the good consequent upon the practice of justice were dependent upon the performance of just actions in every particular case, it is difficult to believe that the consequences of any individual unjust action, considered in itself, could ever be good enough to justify me in performing it. I must, therefore, apply rules of justice in all circumstances, however trivial, and however great the immediate good to be gained by neglecting them.

Thirdly, if Hume did hold the view that we must perform just actions because just actions are necessary if the general practice of justice is to have any value, then his theory is incapable of accounting for the difficulties with which utilitarianism is faced, and for which it was, in part, intended to account. This theory was, in part, intended to explain how we could have a duty to perform some actions the consequences of which were indifferent or positively bad, and it is one of the great merits of the view that we have a duty to perform actions because they are of a sort which would produce good consequences if generally practised, that it does enable us to explain how it is that we have a duty to perform some actions which, in themselves, have bad or indifferent consequences. But the theory that it is our duty to perform just actions because their performance is necessary for the good of justice to be realised does not, in fact, do this. It does not, as does the other theory, admit and account for the fact that we have a duty to perform some actions which do not themselves produce good consequences, for it does not recognise that there are such duties. All that can be said, if we adopt it, is that there are some actions, which seem to produce no good consequences, or even to produce bad consequences, when we take a narrow and restricted view. When we take a more enlarged view, and consider these actions along with other actions of the same sort, it will be seen that, in actual fact, they really do produce good consequences; they produce good consequences because they are one of a set of actions the several performance of which is necessary if a certain good is to be produced. This view, therefore, does not find a place in the utilitarian scheme of duties for our duty to perform actions which do not themselves have good consequences. It merely denies that we have any such duties, and tries to explain how the illusion that we have arises.

Utilitarians—as well as moral philosophers who have not been utilitarians—have not always failed to notice the fact that we think actions are right if they are of a sort which would produce good consequences if generally practised, or are wrong if they are of a sort which would produce bad consequences if other people did the same. Mill, for example, remarked: "In the case of abstinences— indeed of things which people forbear to do from moral considerations, though the consequences in the particular case might be beneficial—it would be unworthy of an intelligent agent not to be consciously aware that the action is of a class which, if practised generally, would be generally injurious, and that this is the ground of the obligation to abstain from it." [7] But utilitarians have not always realised that, in admitting that the performance of such actions is a duty, they are departing from, or, at least, modifying, utilitarianism as it is stated above. And that they are departing from, or modifying, utilitarianism, as it is usually thought of, is clear. For actions which are permissible, according to utilitarianism as I have defined it above, might well not be permissible, according to utilitarianism in this modified form. For it may very well be true of an

[7] John Stuart Mill: *Utilitarianism*, Everyman Edition, pp. 17–18.

action, both that there is no other action within the power of the agent that would produce better consequences than it, and that it is an instance of a class of actions which would produce harmful consequences if they were to be generally performed. In this case, I should, according to utilitarianism as it is normally thought of, be acting rightly if I performed it; whereas, according to this modified form of utilitarianism, I should be acting wrongly.

But the principle that I should perform actions, if they are of a sort which would produce good consequences if generally performed and should refrain from performing actions which would produce bad consequences, if generally performed, is not free from difficulty.

In the first place, the principle is, as it stands, insufficiently precise. An action, it says, is right if it is of a sort which would produce good consequences, if generally practised, and wrong if it is of a sort which would produce harmful consequences, if generally practised. But no action is an instance of just one sort or class of actions; every action is an instance of many such sorts. It may well be that among the many classes of action of which a given action is an instance, there may be some classes which would have good consequences, if generally performed, some classes which would have bad consequences, if generally performed, and yet other classes, the general performance of which would be indifferent. When we say that the consequences, for good or for ill, of the class of actions of which a given action is a member should be taken into account when we are considering whether or not that action ought to be performed, about which of the many classes, of which the action in question is an instance, are we talking? Which of these classes should be considered, when we are wondering whether such an action is a right and proper one for us to do?

Some of the classes, of which it is a member, should not be considered by us because the consequences which they would have, if generally performed, are different from the consequences their subclasses would have, if they were generally performed. Suppose, for example, that a redheaded man with one eye, a wart on his right cheek, and a mermaid tattooed on his left forearm, were to tell a lie on a Tuesday. It might be argued that it was quite permissible for him to have told this lie, because his action in telling the lie belongs to the class of actions performed on a Tuesday, and the consequences of the general performance of actions on a Tuesday is indifferent. But the class of actions performed on a Tuesday is not the sort of class which it is important to consider, when meditating upon the consequences of the general performance of certain classes of actions. For the class of actions performed on a Tuesday contains within itself a number of sub-classes: deceitful actions on a Tuesday, self-sacrificing actions on a Tuesday, revengeful actions on a Tuesday, and so on. The consequences of the general performance of actions in these sub-classes will differ both from one another and from the consequences of the general performance of that wider class which is the genus. Since this is the case, it would be unreasonable for us to consider the consequences of the general performance of actions on a Tuesday. For the consequences of the general practice of lying on a Tuesday are different from those of the general practice of actions of any sort on a Tuesday, and it is the consequences of the general performance of the more specific class of actions which it is important for us to consider.

It can be important for us to consider the consequences of the general performance of a certain class of actions only if that class contains within itself no sub-classes, the consequences of the general practice of which is either better or worse than the consequences of the general practice of actions belonging to it. It would be inaccurate to say that this class is of the wrong sort because it is too generic. For the class of actions performed between 3 p.m. and 3:01 p.m. on Tuesday is a good deal more specific than it is, and yet is of the wrong sort for precisely the same reason.

If, on the other hand—to revert to our original example—we were to consider, not the consequences of the general practice of lying, but the consequences of the general practice of lying by one-eyed, red-headed men, with warts on their right cheeks and mermaids tattooed on their left forearms, then the class of actions we were considering would be a wrong one, but for a different reason. The class of actions performed on Tuesday afternoon was a wrong one to consider, because it could be "relevantly specified"; that is to say, by the addition of characteristics such as "being the telling of a lie" I could obtain a more specific class of actions, the consequences of the general performance of which would be different from the consequences of the general performance of actions belonging to it. The class of actions, "lies told by one-eyed, red-headed men, with warts on their right cheeks, and mermaids tattooed on their left forearms," is a wrong one because it can be "irrelevantly generalised"; that is to say, by subtracting characteristics such as "being an action performed by a one-eyed man" I can obtain more general classes of actions, the consequences of the general performance of which do not differ from the consequences of the general performance of actions belonging to it.

In the second place, the principle seems to rule out as being wrong a number of actions which everybody normally thinks to be permissible, and would make obligatory as duties many actions which people do not normally consider to be such. The principle that I should perform actions, the general practice of which would be beneficial, is often used as an argument for pacifism, and with some plausibility. If everybody were to refrain from participating in wars, there would be no wars; hence it is my duty to refrain from participating in wars, whether anybody else cooperates with me or not. But the same principle can be used to justify actions which even a pacifist would condemn. If nobody were to lay violent hands upon the persons of his neighbours, or upon their property, everyone would live in peace with his fellow men—and what a desirable state of affairs this would be! But must the policeman for this reason refrain from forcibly apprehending the criminal, the judge from sending him to prison, and the gaoler from keeping him there? Similarly, the principle that I should refrain from performing actions which would be harmful if generally performed would make it obligatory for me to refrain from performing many actions which I have, no doubt, a duty not to do. But it would also make it obligatory for me to refrain from performing many actions which we would all regard as being permissible, if not positively as duties. It would make it my duty, for example, not to become a professional philosopher, because, in a world in which everybody became professional philosophers, it would be impossible to survive. The same principle would prohibit entry into almost any trade or profession, with the possible exception of that of agricultural labourer.

But in answering the first difficulty, the means of answering this second difficulty have already been provided. It is true, for example, that if we consider violent actions generally, then, if everybody refrained from violent actions, good consequences would result. But the class of violent actions is not the class which it is important to consider, when we are wondering whether an action is of a sort which would have good or bad consequences if generally performed. The class of violent actions is not the right class for us to consider because it can relevantly be made more specific. It contains within itself, as sub-classes, such species of violent actions as the violence of a parent towards a child, the violence of a policeman towards a criminal, the violence of a criminal towards a householder, the violence of one soldier to another, the violence of one small boy to another small boy. Since the consequences of the general practice of these sub-classes of violent action may be, and very probably are, different from the consequences of the universal practice of violent actions in general, then it is the consequences of the general practice of the species which we should consider, not of the genus. So, too, participation in wars is a class of actions which can be made relevantly more specific, if it is limited by the addition of suitable characteristics. It contains sub-classes, such as participation in wars on behalf of an aggressor, participation in wars on behalf of a country which is resisting aggression, participation in wars as a mercenary on behalf of a country of which one is not a citizen, participation in religious wars, participation in disciplinary wars on behalf of some international authority. Since the consequences of the general performance of these species will differ from the consequences of the general performance of the genus, then it is the species which should be considered, not the genus. To take the third example, if everyone were to become university lecturers, the consequences would, no doubt, be deplorable. But the entering into the profession of university lecturer is a class of actions which contains species such as that of becoming a university lecturer by men who have no aptitude for medicine, no liking for the civil service, and who have a capacity for acquiring and disseminating information which would be unsuitable for schoolchildren, but of not much use or interest to ordinary adults. Becoming a university lecturer is a class of actions which can be relevantly specified, and, since this is so, it is the consequences of the general practice of the species which we should consider, not the consequences of the general practice of the genus.

Actions are right if they are of a sort which would produce good consequences, if generally practised. Now being right is a property of the individual action. Being generally practised (or seldom, or always, or never practised, as the case may be) is a property of the sort of action this action is, or of the class of actions of which it is a member. But of what is producing good consequences a property? When actions of this sort are not generally practised, producing good consequences will, of course, be a property of nothing. But when actions of this sort are generally practised, of what will producing good consequences be a property? Not of the sort, because sorts or classes cannot produce good consequences, or fail to produce them, though instances of the sort or members of the class can. Producing good consequences must, then, be a property of the individual actions. But if we say that every individual action of the sort produces good consequences, then our principle does not meet the difficulty which it was introduced to meet, namely, the difficulty that there are actions which are right, although they do not produce good consequences. Whereas if we say that only some of the individual actions of the sort produce good consequences, we are faced with this perplexing situation: the rightness of some instances of the sort is derived from the good consequences produced by other instances of the sort. We are faced, too, with this further difficulty. A utilitarian, if he is to deserve the name at all, must try to derive the rightness of actions in some way from the good ends which they serve. So it may be objected that, if the general practice of a sort of action produces good consequences, even when some actions of the sort produce no good consequences, or even bad consequences, would not even better consequences be produced if people were to refrain from performing those actions of the sort which did not produce good consequences, and performed only those that did? [8] But if this is the case, then it cannot be argued that the rightness of those actions which do not produce good consequences is dependent on the fact that in some way they serve a

[8] *See* D. G. C. Macnabb: David Hume: His *Theory of Knowledge and Morality*, p. 182.

good end, for this, so far from being a fact, is, as the preceding argument has shown, simply not true.

The argument I have just stated does not, I think, show that the man who holds that our duty to perform a certain action may be founded upon the good consequences of the general performance of similar actions cannot properly be called a utilitarian, but it does serve to elicit an important property which such classes of action must have. Consider, for example, the class of actions "drinking cocoa for breakfast." It may well be that actions of this class would have good consequences, if generally performed, and it may even be that this class of actions cannot relevantly be made more specific, in the way in which I have explained. But even so, the fact, if it is a fact, that actions of this sort would produce good consequences, if they were to be generally performed, could not possibly be an adequate reason for thinking that either I, or anybody else, has a duty to drink cocoa for breakfast. If I have a duty to drink cocoa for breakfast at all, this duty is derived from the effects of drinking cocoa on my health and temper, that is, on the effects of the particular action to be performed, not upon the effects of the general performance of similar actions.

If this is so, then the mere fact that actions of a certain class would have good consequences if they were generally performed cannot be sufficient to make performance of such actions a duty, even when the class in question cannot relevantly be made more specific. Something more is necessary. Actions of the class in question must be so related to one another that, if they are not performed in the majority of cases, then they will not produce good consequences—or, at any rate, not such good consequences—in any. They must be related to one another in such a way that the good consequences produced by those of them which do produce good consequences are dependent upon a sufficient number of those of them which do not have good consequences being performed. Mr. R. F. Harrod, in an excellent article on the subject,[9] has characterised such classes (in the way in which one would expect of an economist) thus: *"There are certain acts which when performed on n similar occasions have consequences more than n times as great*

---

[9] R. F. Harrod: Utilitarianism Revised, *Mind*, 1936.

as those resulting from one performance. And it is in this class of cases that obligations arise." [10] By obligation, apparently, Mr. Harrod does not mean just any sort of obligation. He means our obligation to perform certain actions, although we could produce better consequences by not performing them.

The difference between the view just outlined and the other theory which Hume might have held is this. According to the other theory, the performance of any action was necessary if the others were to produce good consequences. Hence the good consequences produced by the general performance of the class of actions was equally dependent upon the performance of every member of the class. According to the view just outlined, not every member of the class of actions in question must be performed if the others are to continue to have any value. I may omit to perform any one (or any two, or any three) of those actions which themselves produce no good consequences, without detracting from the value of those which do. But if we were to neglect to perform all the actions in the class which themselves had no good consequences, then the good consequences produced by the others would be seriously affected. Hence our objection is answered. Not to perform any one of the actions which themselves produce no good consequences would not detract from the good produced by the general performance of actions of the class, provided that the others continued to be performed. But not to perform any at all would seriously diminish it, if not take it away altogether.

Hence we must perform certain actions, which produce no good consequences, or even harmful consequences themselves, because, if everybody took the liberty of infringing the rule demanding their performance in the same circumstances, its utility would be lost. But we do not think that such rules should be applied in all circumstances. We do not, it is true, think that we should fail to apply a rule, simply because one particular failure to apply it would produce no bad consequences, or even if application of the rule produced harmful consequences, provided that these consequences are not harmful beyond a certain point. But we do not think that such rules should be applied, however disastrous the consequences of

[10] *Op. cit.*, p. 148.

applying them are. We think that, if the consequences of a certain application of a rule are disastrous, or even bad beyond a certain point, then the rule should be set aside in this particular case. In other words, when benevolence conflicts with justice, we do not, as Hume seemed to imply, think that justice should always override benevolence. In what circumstances, then, should justice prevail, and in what circumstances benevolence?

We should, I think, only apply a rule to a hard case if the gain which would result from failing to apply the rule in all cases as hard or harder exceeds the loss which would result from failure to apply the rule to those cases. To suppose that the utility of a rule must be destroyed, or even greatly diminished, by failure to apply it in certain restricted instances is a mistake. If we were only to fail to apply it to the hardest of hard cases, the rule might be neglected so rarely that its utility might be undiminished. It is only when we cease to apply the rule to cases less hard that the utility of the rule is impaired, and, even so, the gain from relieving the hard cases may be sufficient to counterbalance the loss of some of the benefit derived from the general application of the rule. If the gain from relieving the hard cases is only just sufficient to balance the loss of utility to the rule, then it is a matter of indifference whether we apply the rule or not. If the gain is insufficient to do this, then the rule should be applied. Mr. Harrod, in the article I have just mentioned, sums up the matter thus: "A lie is justified when the balance of pain or loss of pleasure is such that, if a lie was told in all circumstances when there was no less a balance of pain or loss of pleasure, the harm due to the total loss of confidence did not exceed the sum of harm due to truthfulness in every case." [11] It should be remembered that, though the gain due to failing to apply a rule to a case which is not very hard is, in respect of every individual failure to apply the rule, smaller than the gain resulting from failure to apply a rule to a case which is very hard, not very hard cases occur much more frequently than very hard cases, and, in this respect, the not very hard cases have the advantage. On the other hand, the fact that not very hard cases are frequent means

[11] *Op. cit.*, p. 149.

that the loss of utility to the rule by failure to apply it to them will be correspondingly greater than the loss of utility caused by failure to apply it to the very hard cases.

Readers will have noticed that this modified form of utilitarianism agrees with intuitionism in the form in which it is held by Sir David Ross in that, according to both him and it, we should not break certain rules simply because the consequences of breaking them are better than the consequences of keeping them. But it is, in one important respect, superior to Sir David Ross's theory. He thinks that we should pay our debt, keep our promises, honour our agreements, and tell the truth even in circumstances when we could produce more good by failing to do so. On the other hand, he quite properly does not hold the extreme view, that these rules should be observed, however great are the advantages of breaking them. In his own language, he thinks that we have a *prima facie* duty to bring about as much good as we can, as well as *prima facie* duties to keep our promises and tell the truth, and so on. When our *prima facie* duty to produce as much good as we can conflicts with our other duties, he thinks that sometimes it is a duty to perform the former *prima facie* duty, sometimes a duty to perform one of the others. But he is quite unable to provide us with any principle which will tell us when we should tell the truth, or keep the promise, and when we should tell the lie, or break the promise, in order to produce good consequences. He is quite sure that the principle by which we decide between these two conflicting rules is not what utilitarianism, as he understands it, says it is. According to the unmodified form of utilitarianism, we should tell the truth only so long as the consequences of truth-telling are better than the consequences of lying. If the consequences of truth-telling are just as good, or just as bad, as the consequences of lying, then it does not matter whether we tell the truth or not. If the consequences of lying are better than the consequences of telling the truth, then we should lie. Sir David Ross, on the other hand, thinks that we should not lie if the consequences of lying are only slightly better than the consequences of telling the truth, but what we should lie, if the consequences of lying are greatly better. But just how much better the consequences of lying must be than the consequences of telling the truth he is unable to tell us. But this modified form of utilitarianism can tell us, and it is, in this respect, if in no other, superior to Sir David Ross's view.

Utilitarianism, in its modified form, may also provide us with the solution to another of Sir David Ross's problems. What happens when, for example, my *prima facie* duty to tell the truth conflicts with my *prima facie* duty to keep my promises? Sir David Ross tells us that, when this happens, it is sometimes my duty to tell the truth, and sometimes my duty to keep my promise. But again, he is unable to provide us with any principle whereby we can decide between such conflicting *prima facie* duties. This, indeed, accords with his general view that, though rules can be given concerning what actions are *prima facie* duties, no rules can be given concerning what actions are duties.

Sir David Ross, though he thinks no principles can be given about duties, thinks that we do at least know enough about them to be able to reject the traditional utilitarian's way of solving the problem. We should not, he thinks, tell the lie and keep the promise, or tell the truth and break the promise, according to which of these two alternatives produce the most good. On this point he is probably right. But, it should be noticed, this is not the principle which the modified form of utilitarianism which we are discussing would recommend. We should not consider just the consequences of telling this lie and keeping this promise, or telling this truth and breaking this promise. We should consider what would be the consequences if everybody were to tell such lies in order to keep such promises or, what comes to the same thing, to break such promises in order to enunciate such truths. It may well be that, after reflection upon the general practice of such actions, we conclude that we should keep the promise and tell the lie, even though the consequences of breaking the promise and telling the truth would be better. It should be remembered, too, that the consequences of the general practice of keeping this sort of promise, or of telling this sort of truth, may differ from the consequences of the general practice of promise-keeping or truth-telling as genera.

So far, so good. But it may well be objected that we have no duty to perform an action simply because it is of a sort which would produce good consequences, if performed by everybody, or to refrain from performing it, because the general performance of it would be bad. Surely, it might be argued, we must be realistic about matters of duty. We should not base our conduct upon what would happen, if certain conditions, which may be unfulfilled, were realised. We should base our conduct upon what, after the fullest consideration possible in the time at our disposal, it seems most likely will happen. If, therefore, I can relieve a hard case by failing to apply a rule of justice, I should do so, even if the consequences of everybody doing the same would be bad, so long as I have reason to suppose that everybody will not do the same. Even if good consequences would be brought about by the general performance of a certain type of action, I have no duty to perform it, so long as I have good reason to believe that actions of that type will not, in fact, be generally performed. This, it might seem, is what Hobbes thought, and Hume —some of the time—because they both thought that we had not a duty to be just in a state of nature, that is, in a state in which nobody else is just. Hume, though he thought that we had no duty to be just in a state of nature, thought that our duty to be benevolent was still incumbent upon us, for our duty to be benevolent, unlike our duty to be just, is in no way dependent upon the performance of benevolent actions by other people. Hence, in a state of nature, I have a duty to be benevolent to my fellows and to women[12] and domestic animals, though I have no duty to be just to them.

Mr. Harrod has an answer to this problem, which does not seem to me to be satisfactory. He says:

> I believe that, where the practice is not general, a second refining process is required. Will the gain due to its application by all conscientious, that is, moral, people *only* be sufficient to offset the loss which the crude utilitarian principle registers? It may be objected that there are no moral people. To meet this, for the word moral in the second refining principle, say people sufficiently moral to act disinterestedly in this kind of case.[13]

[12] "In many nations the female sex are reduced to like slavery, and are rendered incapable of all property, in opposition to their lordly masters. But though the males, when united, have in all countries bodily force sufficient to maintain this severe tyranny, yet such are the insinuation, address and charms of their fair companions, that women are commonly able to break the confederacy, and share with the other sex in all the rights and privileges of society." L. A. Selby-Bigge: *Hume's Enquiries*, p. 191.

[13] *Op. cit.*, p. 151.

This answer, however, cannot be accepted. It is being objected that we do not have a duty to apply the principle where nobody else applies it, and Mr. Harrod replies that we have a duty to apply it if there are enough moral people to do likewise. But wherein lies their morality? In applying the principle? But then, they cannot be moral if the principle is not moral, and it is the morality of the principle which is being called in question—and actually, by Mr. Harrod himself, set aside, in favour of the principle as doubly refined. And how many people are there moral enough to apply the principle in a state of nature? Surely, none at all, for a state of nature is defined as one in which there is nobody moral enough to apply the principle.

I think that Mr. Harrod, under the guise of defending the principle that the good or bad consequences of the general performance of a certain type of action should be considered, is really siding with its opponents. For I think that he really believes that it is important to know how many people there are sufficiently moral to apply the principle which I apply, because he thinks that it is important for me to know how likely it is that other people will apply the principle, before I can make up my mind whether I myself have a duty to apply it. But this is just what opponents of the principle think. They think that I have not a duty to be just rather than to relieve a hard case, even if the consequences which would result if everybody were to be unjust in similar cases would be bad, so long as I have reason to believe that other people will not be unjust in similar cases. They think that I have not a duty to be just in a state of nature, even though good consequences would result if everybody were to be just, because I have reason to believe that I shall be alone in my practice of justice.

To the man who objects that one may be unjust to relieve a hard case, even if such an action would have bad consequences if everybody else were to do the same, provided that I have reason to believe that nobody else will do the same, one is inclined to make the following answer. I am not in a better position to estimate what other people will do than they are to estimate what I will do and, if everybody were to relieve hard cases because they thought that it was unlikely that other people would do the same, bad consequences would result. We are inclined to say, if nobody were just in a state of nature, because they thought it unlikely that justice would also be practised by others, then we would never get out of a state of nature. If it be objected that we were never in a state of nature, it may be replied that we are all in a state of nature with regard to some things. Men may not be in a state of nature with regard to debt-paying, nor Englishmen with regard to queueing, but nations are in a state of nature with regard to international agreements, and housewives are, very likely, in a state of nature with regard to saving scrap, when they are told that, if everybody handed in their old dustbin lids, enough metal would be saved to build a battleship.

But, of course, in making these answers, we are not justifying the principle—though we are making it more plausible—for we are falling back on the very principle we are trying to justify. Nor is it possible to justify the principle. If it is true, then it must be accepted as true without reason, though this does not mean that it is irrational to accept it. In this respect it is like any fundamental moral principle, so the fact that it cannot be justified must not be held against it.

But the probability or otherwise of other people doing what I do does have a bearing on my duty to do an action (or to refrain from doing it) if it would have good (or bad) consequences if everybody else did the same. It is true that, if I only have good reason for thinking that other people will not do what I do, then my duty to be just in a hard case still applies. For other people's reasons for thinking that theirs will not be the general practice are as good as mine and, if everybody failed to apply a rule in a hard case merely because they had good reasons for thinking that others would not do the same, bad consequences would result. But if I had conclusive reasons for thinking that other people would not do the same, then it would be my duty to relieve the hard case. For only one person can have conclusive reasons for thinking that others will not relieve the hard cases he relieves, and, from one person's relieving hard cases, no disastrous consequences follow. Similarly, in a state of nature, if I only have good reasons for thinking that others will not apply the rules I apply, my duty to apply these rules remains. But if I have conclusive reasons for thinking that others will not apply the rules I apply, my duty to apply them ceases. For if everybody were to fail to apply these rules only in circumstances in which they knew that nobody else would do the same, no bad consequences would follow. If these two examples seem artificial, this is only because I have considered extreme cases. It is unlikely that I should know that nobody but I will fail to apply a rule of justice in a hard case, and it is unlikely that I should know that no one but I will be just in a state bordering upon a state of nature. But I may sometimes know that the majority of people will not apply a rule to cases as hard as the case to which I fail to apply it, or know that the majority of people are too short sighted and unrestrained to apply a rule of justice in cases where others do not. In such cases, supposing imitation by a minority of people only is not sufficient to produce any good (or bad) effects, my duty to apply the rule ceases.

This, however, is not an exception to the principles already expounded, but a consequence of them. What I am saying, in others words, is that my knowledge of the behaviour of other people is a characteristic which relevantly specifies the class of actions the consequences of the general practice of which it is my duty to consider. I have a duty to perform a certain action, although believing that other people will not perform it, because, if everybody who believed that other people would not perform it were to do similar actions, good consequences would result. I have not a duty to perform an action, when knowing that other people will not do likewise because, if people performed similar actions only when they knew no one else would do the same, no good consequences would follow.

My duty to perform actions of a sort which would have good consequences if they were generally practised will thus depend, in some measure, upon my ignorance of the behaviour of other people. I must not, for example, turn aside from applying a principle of justice in a hard case when I do not know that other people will not do the same, because I have every reason to believe that they will have much the same reasons for failing to apply a rule of justice to similar hard cases as I have for failing to apply it to this one, and because, if everybody were to do what I propose doing, disastrous consequences would follow. But, if I were omniscient about the behaviour of other people, then it would be my duty to do that action, which itself has good consequences. But this is not because the principle that we ought always to perform those actions which would have good consequences, if generally performed, and to refrain from performing those actions which would have bad consequences, if generally performed, is not applicable to people who have complete knowledge of the behaviour of others. It is because, to people who have complete knowledge of the behaviour of others, the two principles, that we should perform those actions which themselves have good consequences, and that we should perform those actions which are of a sort which would have good consequences, if practised generally, enjoin the same actions. If everybody having complete knowledge of the behaviour of other people were to perform those actions which themselves had good consequences, good consequences would result; whereas, if all people having complete knowledge of the behavior of other people were to perform those actions which themselves had bad consequences, bad consequences would result. In the case of people having complete knowledge of the behaviour of others, the unmodified utilitarian principle falls under the modified principle as a special case, and an omniscient being would be justified in acting upon it, though beings like ourselves would not.[14] This does not mean, of course, that the two principles are identical. They would not be identical, even if they always enjoined identical actions, whereas they only do this in very special circumstances. Even when they enjoin identical actions, it is the modified utilitarian principle which is obligatory. The unmodified principle derives its obligatoriness from its accordance with the modified principle, and it is not obligatory in its own right.

It will not have escaped the reader, and it certainly did not escape Mr. Harrod, that there is some connection between the modified utilitarian principle and the Kantian categorical imperative. Now

---

[14] Cf. Butler: *Works, Gladstone's Edition,* Vol. II, p. 190 n. "For instance: As we are not competent judges, what is upon the whole for the good of the world, there may be other immediate ends appointed us to pursue, besides that one of doing good, or producing happiness. Though the good of the creation be the only end of the Author of it, yet he may have laid us under particular obligations, which we may discern and feel ourselves under, quite distinct from a perception, that the observance or violation of them is for the happiness or misery of our fellow creatures." Also C. D. Broad: *Five Types of Ethical Theory,* pp. 81–82.

I do not think that the modified utilitarian principle can be deduced, as Kant thought moral principles could be deduced from the idea of law in general. The claim that moral principles can be deduced from the idea of law in general depends, I think, upon the claim that there is only one set of principles upon which, taken singly or together, it is possible for everybody to act, coupled with a definition of "law" according to which no principle upon which everybody cannot act can properly be said to be a law. It does not seem to me that the claim that there is only one set of principles upon which everyone can act is justified. A universe in which everybody acted morally is perfectly conceivable, but so is a universe in which everybody acted morally, with the exception that everybody committed suicide at the age of fifty. The fact that it is possible for everybody to commit suicide at the age of fifty (and, at the same time, to be moral in other respects) does not seem to me to show that it is obligatory, or even permissible, to do this.

Nor do I think that imperfect duties can be derived from the impossibility of one's being able to will that everybody should fail to perform an imperfect duty. First of all it is not clear to me that this is impossible. If a man were sufficiently callous to murder his own wife, might he not be sufficiently callous, supposing he had the power, to will that other men should murder theirs? Besides, why cannot one will that everybody should fail to perform an (imperfect) duty? Not because of the moral repugnance such general negligence would cause us; Kant is supposed to be giving our inability to will that an action should be generally performed as a reason for thinking that it is wrong, and not *vice versa*. Are we unable to will general neglect of a duty, because such neglect would be contrary to our interest? Kant speaks as if I cannot will that people should not help others in distress, because, in that case, no one would help me when I am in distress. But, if the fact that an action has consequences which are detrimental to my interest is a bad reason for thinking that it is wrong, surely the fact that I cannot, from self-interest, will its universal performance, is a worse one.

But the modified utilitarian principle, though it is not impossible for everybody to fail to act upon it, and though it is not impossible, though it may be immoral, for one to will that everybody should transgress it, does conform to some suggestions which may be found

in the works of Kant. First of all, the unmodified utilitarian principle is self-defeating, whereas the modified principle is not. If
everybody were to act upon the unmodified utilitarian principle,
everybody would fail to apply rules of justice to certain hard cases,
and bad consequences would result. But the purpose of the people
who applied the unmodified utilitarian principle would be to produce good consequences, and so the general application of the rule
they were practising would defeat the ends which determined them
to adopt it.

Secondly, suppose that I apply the unmodified utilitarian principle to a certain case, knowing that, if other people apply the
modified principle, I can produce good consequences by doing so.
In this case, my conduct, though beneficial is, in a certain sense,
inconsistent. It is not inconsistent in the sense that it is impossible
for me to do what I do, nor in the sense that it is impossible for
everybody to do what I do, nor in the sense that it is impossible for
me to do what I do, while others do what they do. My principle is
inconsistent with theirs in the sense that both of them could not
be acted upon by everybody or, for that matter, by anybody. Since
my own principle would be self-defeating if universally adopted,
I do not regard it as fit for application by everybody, but take the
liberty of allowing myself to make an exception to the ones that I do
regard as suitable. Should it be argued, on behalf of a more nearly
Kantian position, that my principle is really "Apply the unmodified
utilitarian formula, so long as everybody else applies the modified
formula," and that this principle cannot be acted upon by everybody. I reply that this argument rests upon a confusion. A judge is
applying the principle "Condemn all murderers" just as much when
he frees an innocent man as when he sentences a murderer. Similarly,
the rest of the world, which is applying the modified utilitarian
formula, may just as much be acting on the principle "Apply the
unmodified utilitarian formula, so long as everybody else applies
the modified formula" as am I, who apply the unmodified formula.
What is impossible, is not that everybody should apply this principle, but that it should ever enjoin more than one person to apply
the unmodified utilitarian formula.

The result is some reconciliation between the doctrine of Kant
and the teleological ethical principles which he despised. An end,

we must say, stands in much the same relation to the morality of principles as do the "facts" in relation to the truth of propositions, and we can no more decide what principles are and are not moral, by means of consistency alone, without reference to ends, than we can settle what propositions are true, by means of consistency alone, without reference to "facts." But though the fitness of any principle to be a moral principle cannot be decided without some reference to an end, the principle must be such that this end is harmoniously and coherently realised by its universal application and, if it can be successfully applied only by a given individual who relies upon the methods of others being more orthodox than his own, the principle is not one which deserves to be called "moral."

In other words, the unmodified utilitarian principle is not eligible to be part of a system of universal legislation, whereas the modified principle is, though it is not the only principle which is. In this respect the modified principles does, while the unmodified principle does not, conform to one of the conditions which any principle must fulfill if it is to be regarded as a principle on which we ought to act, and this condition it is one of Kant' great merits to have emphasised. No principle is fit to be a moral principle unless it is fit that it should be universally adopted and universally applied, though a principle may be unfit for universal adoption, even where universal adoption is logically possible. Our attitude to a principle cannot be a distinctively moral one unless we are prepared to accept, and sometimes to recommend, its universal application. The unmodified utilitarian principle conforms to neither of these two conditions. It is not fit for universal adoption, because the very grounds, namely, that it serves a good end, which recommend its application by one person, prohibit its application by everybody. And our attitude to it cannot be a moral one. For we can be prepared to apply it ourselves only so long as others do not, and hence we cannot possibly be prepared to recommend that it be adopted by others besides ourselves.

J. J. C. SMART

Extreme and Restricted
Utilitarianism

I

Utilitarianism is the doctrine that the rightness of actions is to be
judged by their consequences. What do we mean by "actions" here?
Do we mean particular actions or do we mean classes of actions?
According to which way we interpret the word "actions" we get two
different theories, both of which merit the appellation "utilitarian."

(1) If by "actions" we mean particular individual actions we get
the sort of doctrine held by Bentham, Sidgwick, and Moore. According to this doctrine we test individual actions by their consequences,
and general rules, like "keep promises," are mere rules of thumb
which we use only to avoid the necessity of estimating the probable
consequences of our actions at every step. The rightness or wrongness of keeping a promise on a particular occasion depends only on
the goodness or badness of the consequences of keeping or of breaking the promise on that particular occasion. Of course part of the
consequences of breaking the promise, and a part to which we will
normally ascribe decisive importance, will be the weakening of faith
in the institution of promising. However, if the goodness of the consequences of breaking the rule is *in toto* greater than the goodness

* From *Philosophical Quarterly*, 6 (1956), 345–54, by permission of the *Philosophical Quarterly*, the Oxford University Press, and the author. Based on a
paper read to the Victorian Branch of the Australasian Association of Psychol-
ogy and Philosophy, October 1955.

of the consequences of keeping it, then we must break the rule, irrespective of whether the goodness of the consequences of *everybody's* obeying the rule is or is not greater than the consequences of *everybody's* breaking it. To put it shortly, rules do not matter, save *per accidens* as rules of thumb and as *de facto* social institutions with which the utilitarian has to reckon when estimating consequences. I shall call this doctrine "extreme utilitarianism."

(2) A more modest form of utilitarianism has recently become fashionable. The doctrine is to be found in Toulmin's book *The Place of Reason in Ethics,* in Nowell-Smith's *Ethics* (though I think Nowell-Smith has qualms), in John Austin's *Lectures on Jurisprudence* (Lecture II), and even in J. S. Mill, if Urmson's interpretation of him is correct (*Philosophical Quarterly,* Vol. 3, pp. 33–39, 1953). Part of its charm is that it appears to resolve the dispute in moral philosophy between intuitionists and utilitarians in a way which is very neat. The above philosophers hold, or seem to hold, that moral rules are more than rules of thumb. In general the rightness of an action is *not* to be tested by evaluating its consequences but only by considering whether or not it falls under a certain rule. Whether the rule is to be considered an acceptable moral rule, is, however, to be decided by considering the consequences of adopting the rule. Broadly, then, actions are to be tested by rules and rules by consequences. The only cases in which we must test an individual action directly by its consequences are (a) when the action comes under two different rules, one of which enjoins it and one of which forbids it, and (b) when there is no rule whatever that governs the given case. I shall call this doctrine "restricted utilitarianism."

It should be noticed that the distinction I am making cuts across, and is quite different from, the distinction commonly made between hedonistic and ideal utilitarianism. Bentham was an extreme hedonistic utilitarian and Moore an extreme ideal utilitarian, and Toulmin (perhaps) could be classified as a restricted ideal utilitarian. A hedonistic utilitarian holds that the goodness of the consequences of an action is a function only of their pleasurableness and an ideal utilitarian, like Moore, holds that pleasurableness is not even a necessary condition of goodness. Mill seems, if we are to take his remarks about higher and lower pleasures seriously, to be neither a pure hedonistic nor a pure ideal utilitarian. He seems to hold that pleasurableness is a necessary condition for goodness, but that goodness is a function of other qualities of mind as well. Perhaps we can call him a quasi-ideal utilitarian. When we say that a state of mind is good I take it that we are expressing some sort of *rational preference*. When we say that it is pleasurable I take it that we are saying that it is enjoyable, and when we say that something is a higher pleasure I take it that we are saying that it is more truly, or more deeply, enjoyable. I am doubtful whether "more deeply enjoyable" does not just mean "more enjoyable, even though not more enjoyable on a first look," and so I am doubtful whether quasi-ideal utilitarianism, and possibly ideal utilitarianism too, would not collapse into hedonistic utilitarianism on a closer scrutiny of the logic of words like "preference," "pleasure," "enjoy," "deeply enjoy," and so on. However, it is beside the point of the present paper to go into these questions. I am here concerned only with the issue between extreme and restricted utilitarianism and am ready to concede that both forms of utilitarianism can be either hedonistic or nonhedonistic.

The issue between extreme and restricted utilitarianism can be illustrated by considering the remark "But suppose everyone did the same." (Cf. A. K. Stout's article in *The Australasian Journal of Philosophy*, Vol. 32, pp. 1–29.) Stout distinguishes two forms of the universalisation principle, the causal form and the hypothetical form. To say that you ought not to do an action A because it would have bad results if everyone (or many people) did action A may be merely to point out that while the action A would otherwise be the optimific one, nevertheless when you take into account that doing A will probably cause other people to do A too, you can see that A is not, on a broad view, really optimific. If this causal influence could be avoided (as may happen in the case of a secret desert island promise) then we would disregard the universalisation principle. This is the causal form of the principle. A person who accepted the universalisation principle in its hypothetical form would be one who was concerned only with what would happen *if* everyone did the action A: he would be totally unconcerned with the question of whether in fact everyone would do the action A. That is, he might say that it would be wrong not to vote because it would have bad results if everyone took this attitude, and he would be totally unmoved by arguments purporting to show that my refusing to vote has no effect whatever on other people's propensity to vote. Making use of Stout's distinction, we can say that an extreme utilitarian would apply the universalisation principle in the causal form, while a restricted utilitarian would apply it in the hypothetical form.

How are we to decide the issue between extreme and restricted utilitarianism? I wish to repudiate at the outset that milk and water approach which describes itself sometimes as "investigating what is implicit in the common moral consciousness" and sometimes as "investigating how people ordinarily talk about morality." We have only to read the newspaper correspondence about capital punishment or about what should be done with Formosa to realise that the common moral consciousness is in part made up of superstitious elements, of morally bad elements, and of logically confused elements. I address myself to good hearted and benevolent people and so I hope that if we rid ourselves of the logical confusion the superstitious and morally bad elements will largely fall away. For even among good hearted and benevolent people it is possible to find superstitious and morally bad reasons for moral beliefs. These superstitious and morally bad reasons hide behind the protective screen of logical confusion. With people who are not logically confused but who are openly superstitious or morally bad I can of course do nothing. That is, our ultimate pro-attitudes may be different. Nevertheless I propose to rely on *my own* moral consciousness and to appeal to *your* moral consciousness and to forget about what people ordinarily say. "The obligation to obey a rule," says Nowell-Smith (*Ethics,* p. 239), "does not, *in the opinion of ordinary men,*" (my italics) "rest on the beneficial consequences of obeying it in a particular case." What does this prove? Surely it is more than likely that ordinary men are confused here. Philosophers should be able to examine the question more rationally.

II

For an extreme utilitarian moral rules are rules of thumb. In practice the extreme utilitarian will mostly guide his conduct by appealing to the rules ("do not lie," "do not break promises," *etc.*) of common sense morality. This is not because there is anything sacrosanct in the rules themselves but because he can argue that probably he will most often act in an extreme utilitarian way if he does not think as a utilitarian. For one thing, actions have frequently to be done in a hurry. Imagine a man seeing a person drowning. He jumps in and rescues him. There is no time to reason the matter out, but usually this will be the course of action which an extreme utilitarian would recommend if he did reason the matter out. If, however, the man drowning had been drowning in a river near Berchtesgaden in 1938, and if he had had the well known black forelock and moustache of Adolf Hitler, an extreme utilitarian would, if he had time, work out the probability of the man's being the villainous dictator, and if the probability were high enough he would, on extreme utilitarian grounds, leave him to drown. The rescuer, however, has not time. He trusts to his instincts and dives in and rescues the man. And this trusting to instincts and to moral rules can be justified on extreme utilitarian grounds. Furthermore, an extreme utilitarian who knew that the drowning man was Hitler would nevertheless praise the rescuer, not condemn him. For by praising the man he is strengthening a courageous and benevolent disposition of mind, and in general this disposition has great positive utility. (Next time, perhaps, it will be Winston Churchill that the man saves!) We must never forget that an extreme utilitarian may praise actions which he knows to be wrong. Saving Hitler was wrong, but it was a member of a class of actions which are generally right, and the motive to do actions of this class is in general an optimific one. In considering questions of praise and blame it is not the expediency of the praised or blamed action that is at issue, but the expediency of the praise. It can be expedient to praise an inexpedient action and inexpedient to praise an expedient one.

Lack of time is not the only reason why an extreme utilitarian may, on extreme utilitarian principles, trust to rules of common sense morality. He knows that in particular cases where his own interests are involved his calculations are likely to be biased in his own favour. Suppose that he is unhappily married and is deciding whether to get divorced. He will in all probability greatly exaggerate his own unhappiness (and possibly his wife's) and greatly underestimate the harm done to his children by the break up of the family. He will probably also underestimate the likely harm done by the weakening of the general faith in marriage vows. So probably he will come to the correct extreme utilitarian conclusion if he does not in this instance think as an extreme utilitarian but trusts to common sense morality.

There are many more and subtle points that could be made in connection with the relation between extreme utilitarianism and the morality of common sense. All those that I have just made and many more will be found in Book IV, Chapters 3–5 of Sidgwick's *Methods of Ethics.* I think that this book is the best book ever written on ethics, and that these chapters are the best chapters of the book. As they occur so near the end of a very long book they are unduly neglected. I refer the reader, then, to Sidgwick for the classical exposition of the relation between (extreme) utilitarianism and the morality of common sense. One further point raised by Sidgwick in this connection is whether an (extreme) utilitarian ought on (extreme) utilitarian principles to propagate (extreme) utilitarianism among the public. As most people are not very philosophical and not good at empirical calculations, it is probable that they will most often act in an extreme utilitarian way if they do not try to think as extreme utilitarians. We have seen how easy it would be to misapply the extreme utilitarian criterion in the case of divorce. Sidgwick seems to think it quite probable that an extreme utilitarian should not propagate his doctrine too widely. However, the great danger to humanity comes nowadays on the plane of public morality—not private morality. There is a greater danger to humanity from the hydrogen bomb than from an increase of the divorce rate, regrettable though that might be, and there seems no doubt that extreme utilitarianism makes for good sense in international relations. When France walked out of the United Nations because she did not wish Morocco discussed, she said that she was within her rights because Morocco and Algiers are part of her metropolitan territory and nothing to do with U.N. This was clearly a legalistic if not superstitious argument. We should not be concerned with the so-called "rights" of France or any other country but with whether the cause of humanity would best be served by discussing Morocco in U.N. (I am not saying that the answer to this is "Yes." There are good grounds for supposing that more harm than good would come by such a discussion.) I myself have no hesitation in saying that on extreme utilitarian principles we ought to propagate extreme utilitarianism as widely as possible. But Sidgwick had respectable reasons for suspecting the opposite.

The extreme utilitarian, then, regards moral rules as rules of thumb and as sociological facts that have to be taken into account when deciding what to do, just as facts of any other sort have to be taken into account. But in themselves they do not justify any action.

III

The restricted utilitarian regards moral rules as more than rules of thumb for short-circuiting calculations of consequences. Generally, he argues, consequences are not relevant at all when we are deciding what to do in a particular case. In general, they are relevant only to deciding what rules are good reasons for acting in a certain way in particular cases. This doctrine is possibly a good account of how the modern unreflective twentieth century Englishman often thinks about morality, but surely it is monstrous as an account of how it is most rational to think about morality. Suppose that there is a rule R and that in 99 per cent of cases the best possible results are obtained by acting in accordance with R. Then clearly R is a useful rule of thumb; if we have not time or are not impartial enough to assess the consequences of an action it is an extremely good bet that the thing to do is to act in accordance with R. But is it not monstrous to suppose that if we *have* worked out the consequences and if we have perfect faith in the impartiality of our calculations, and if we *know* that in this instance to break R will have better results than to keep it, we should nevertheless obey the rule? Is it not to erect R into a sort of idol if we keep it when breaking it will prevent, say, some avoidable misery? Is not this a form of superstitious rule-worship (easily explicable psychologically) and not the rational thought of a philosopher?

The point may be made more clearly if we consider Mill's comparison of moral rules to the tables in the nautical almanack. (*Utilitarianism,* Everyman Edition, pp. 22–23.) This comparison of Mill's is adduced by Urmson as evidence that Mill was a restricted utilitarian, but I do not think that it will bear this interpretation at all. (Though I quite agree with Urmson that many other things said by Mill are in harmony with restricted rather than extreme utilitarianism. Probably Mill had never thought very much about the distinction and was arguing for utilitarianism, restricted or extreme, against other and quite nonutilitarian forms of moral argument.) Mill says: "Nobody argues that the art of navigation is not founded on astronomy, because sailors cannot wait to calculate the Nautical Almanack. Being rational creatures, they go out upon the sea of life with their minds made up on the common questions of right and wrong, as well as on many of the far more difficult questions of wise and foolish. . . . Whatever we adopt as the fundamental principle of morality, we require subordinate principles to apply it by." Notice that this is, as it stands, only an argument for subordinate principles as rules of thumb. The example of the nautical almanack is misleading because the information given in the almanack is in all cases the same as the information one would get if one made a long and laborious calculation from the original astronomical data on which the almanack is founded. Suppose, however, that astronomy were different. Suppose that the behaviour of the sun, moon and planets was very nearly as it is now, but that on rare occasions there were peculiar irregularities and discontinuities, so that the almanack gave us rules of the form "in 99 per cent of cases where the observations are such and such you can deduce that your position is so and so." Furthermore, let us suppose that there were methods which enabled us, by direct and laborious calculation from the original astronomical data, not using the rough and ready tables of the almanack, to get our correct position in 100 per cent of cases. Seafarers might use the almanack because they never had time for the long calculations and they were content with a 99 per cent chance of success in calculating their positions. Would it not be absurd, however, if they *did* make the direct calculation, and finding that it disagreed with the almanack calculation, nevertheless they ignored it and stuck to the almanack conclusion? Of course the case would be altered if there were a high enough probability of making slips in the direct calculation: then we might stick to the almanack result, liable to error though we knew it to be, simply because the direct calculation would be open to error for a different reason, the fallibility of the computer. This would be analogous to the case of the extreme utilitarian who abides by the conventional rule against the dictates of his utilitarian calculations simply because he thinks that his calculations are probably affected by personal bias. But if the navigator were sure of his direct calculations would he not be foolish to abide by his almanack? I conclude, then, that if we change our suppositions about astronomy and the almanack (to which there are no exceptions) to bring the case into line with that of morality (to whose rules there are exceptions), Mill's example loses its appearance of supporting the restricted form of utilitarianism. Let me say once more that I am not here concerned with how ordinary men think about morality but with how they ought to think. We could quite well imagine a race of sailors who acquired a superstitious reverence for their almanack, even though it was only right in 99 per cent of cases, and who indignantly threw overboard any man who mentioned the possibility of a direct calculation. But would this behaviour of the sailors be rational?

Let us consider a much discussed sort of case in which the extreme utilitarian might go against the conventional moral rule. I have promised to a friend, dying on a desert island from which I am subsequently rescued, that I will see that his fortune (over which I have control) is given to a jockey club. However, when I am rescued I decide that it would be better to give the money to a hospital, which can do more good with it. It may be argued that I am wrong to give the money to the hospital. But why? (a) The hospital can do more good with the money than the jockey club can. (b) The present case is unlike most cases of promising in that no one except me knows about the promise. In breaking the promise I am doing so with complete secrecy and am doing nothing to weaken the general faith in promises. That is, a factor, which would normally keep the extreme utilitarian from promise breaking even in otherwise unoptimific cases, does not at present operate. (c) There is no doubt a slight weakening in my own character as an habitual promise keeper, and moreover psychological tensions will be set up in me every time I am asked what the man made me promise him to do. For clearly I shall have to say that he made me promise to give the money to the hospital, and, since I am an habitual truth teller, this will go very much against the grain with me. Indeed I am pretty sure that in practice I myself would keep the promise. But we are not discussing what my moral habits would probably make me do; we are discussing what I ought to do. Moreover, we must not forget that even if it would be most rational of me to give the money to the hospital it would also be most rational of you to punish or condemn me if you did, most improbably, find out the truth (*e.g.* by finding a note washed ashore in a bottle). Furthermore, I would agree that though it was most rational of me to give the money to the hospital it would be most rational of you to condemn me for it. We revert again to Sidgwick's distinction between the utility of the action and the utility of the praise of it.

Many such issues are discussed by A. K. Stout in the article to which I have already referred. I do not wish to go over the same ground again, especially as I think that Stout's arguments support my own point of view. It will be useful, however, to consider one other example that he gives. Suppose that during hot weather there is an edict that no water must be used for watering gardens. I have a garden and I reason that most people are sure to obey the edict, and that as the amount of water that I use will be by itself negligible no harm will be done if I use the water secretly. So I do use the water, thus producing some lovely flowers which give happiness to various people. Still, you may say, though the action was perhaps optimific, it was unfair and wrong.

There are several matters to consider. Certainly my action should be condemned. We revert once more to Sidgwick's distinction. A right action may be rationally condemned. Furthermore, this sort of offence is normally found out. If I have a wonderful garden when everybody else's is dry and brown there is only one explanation. So if I water my garden I am weakening my respect for law and order, and as this leads to bad results an extreme utilitarian would agree that I was wrong to water the garden. Suppose now that the case is altered and that I can keep the thing secret: there is a secluded part of the garden where I grow flowers which I give away anonymously to a home for old ladies. Are you still so sure that I did the wrong thing by watering my garden? However, this is still a weaker case than that of the hospital and the jockey club. There will be tensions set up within myself: my secret knowledge that I have broken the rule will make it hard for me to exhort others to keep the rule. These psychological ill effects in myself may be not inconsiderable: directly and indirectly they may lead to harm which is at least of the same order as the happiness that the old ladies get from the flowers. You can see that on an extreme utilitarian view there are two sides to the question.

So far I have been considering the duty of an extreme utilitarian in a predominantly nonutilitarian society. The case is altered if we consider the extreme utilitarian who lives in a society every member, or most members, of which can be expected to reason as he does. Should he water his flowers now? (Granting, what is doubtful, that in the case already considered he would have been right to water his flowers.) A simple argument, employing the game-theoretical concept of a mixed strategy, suggests that each extreme utilitarian should give himself a very small probability (say be tossing dice) of watering his garden. Suppose that there are m potential garden waterers and that $f(n)$ is the damage done by exactly n people watering their gardens. Now if each of them gives himself a probability p of watering his garden it is easy to calculate, in terms of p, the probabilities p_1, p_2, ... p_m of 1, 2, ... m persons respectively watering their gardens. Let a be the benefit to each gardener of watering his garden. Then if V is the total probable benefit to the community of gardeners we have

$$V = p_1 (a - f(1)) + p_2 (2a - f(2)) + \ldots p_m (ma - f(m))$$

Assuming that numerical values can be given to a and to values of the function $f(n)$ we calculate the value of p for which $\dfrac{dV}{dp} = 0$. This gives the value of p which maximises the total probable benefit. In practical cases of course numerical values of $f(n)$ and a can not be determined, but a good approximation can usually be got by taking p as equal to zero. However the mathematical analysis is of theoretical interest for the discussion of utilitarianism. Too many writers mistakenly suppose that the only two relevant alternatives are that no one does something and that everyone does it.

I now pass on to a type of case which may be thought to be the trump card of restricted utilitarianism. Consider the rule of the road. It may be said that since all that matters is that everyone should do the same it is indifferent which rule we have, "go on the left hand side" or "go on the right hand side." Hence the only *reason* for going on the left hand side in British countries is that this is the rule. Here the rule does seem to be a reason, in itself, for acting in a certain way. I wish to argue against this. The rule in itself is not a reason for our actions. We would be perfectly justified in going on the right hand side if (a) we knew that the rule was to go on the left hand side, and (b) we were in a country peopled by super-anarchists who always on principle did the opposite of what they were told. This shows that the rule does not give us a reason for acting so much as an indication of the probable actions of others, which helps us to find out what would be our own most rational course of action. If we are in a country not peopled by anarchists, but by nonanarchist extreme Utilitarians, we expect, other things being equal, that they will keep rules laid down for them. Knowledge of the rule enables us to predict their behaviour and to harmonise our own actions with theirs. The rule "keep to the left hand side," then, is not a logical *reason* for action but an anthropological *datum* for planning actions.

I conclude that in every case if there is a rule R the keeping of which is in general optimific, but such that in a special sort of circumstances the optimific behaviour is to break R, then in these circumstances we should break R. Of course we must consider all the less obvious effects of breaking R, such as reducing people's faith in the moral order, before coming to the conclusion that to break R is right: in fact we shall rarely come to such a conclusion. Moral rules, on the extreme utilitarian view, are rules of thumb only, but they are not bad rules of thumb. But if we *do* come to the conclusion that we should break the rule and if we have weighed in the balance our own fallibility and liability to personal bias, what good reason remains for keeping the rule? I can understand "it is optimific" as a reason for action, but why should "it is a member of a class of actions which are usually optimific" or "it is a member of a class of actions which as a class are more optimific than any alternative general class" be a good reason? You might as well say that a person ought to be picked to play for Australia just because all his brothers have been, or that the Australian team should be composed entirely of the Harvey family because this would be better than composing it entirely of any other family. The extreme utilitarian does not appeal to artificial feelings, but only to our feelings of benevolence, and what better feelings can there be to appeal to? Admittedly we can have a pro-attitude to anything, even to rules, but such artificially begotten pro-attitudes smack of superstition. Let us get down to realities, human happiness and misery, and make these the objects of our pro-attitudes and anti-attitudes.

The restricted utilitarian might say that he is talking only of *morality*, not of such things as rules of the road. I am not sure how far this objection, if valid, would affect my argument, but in any case I would reply that as a philosopher I conceive of ethics as the study of how it would be *most rational* to act. If my opponent wishes to restrict the word "morality" to a narrower use he can have the word. The fundamental question is the question of rationality of action *in general*. Similarly if the restricted utilitarian were to appeal to ordinary usage and say "it might be most rational to leave Hitler to drown but it would surely not be *wrong* to rescue him," I should again let him have the words "right" and "wrong" and should stick to "rational" and "irrational." We already saw that it would be rational to praise Hitler's rescuer, even though it would have been most rational not to have rescued Hitler. In ordinary language, no doubt, "right" and "wrong" have not only the meaning "most rational to do" and "not most rational to do" but also have the meaning "praiseworthy" and "not praiseworthy." Usually to the utility of an action corresponds utility of praise of it, but as we saw, this is not always so. Moral language could thus do with tidying up, for example by reserving "right" for "most rational" and "good" as an epithet of praise for the motive from which the action sprang. It would be more becoming in a philosopher to try to iron out illogicalities in moral language and to make suggestions for its reform than to use it as a court of appeal whereby to perpetuate confusions.

One last defence of restricted utilitarianism might be as follows. "Act optimifically" might be regarded as itself one of the rules of our system (though it would be odd to say that this rule was justified by its optimificality). According to Toulmin (*The Place of Reason in Ethics*, pp. 146–48) if "keep promises," say, conflicts with another rule we are allowed to argue the case on its merits, as if we were extreme utilitarians. If "act optimifically" is itself one of our rules then there will always be a conflict of rules whenever to keep a rule is not itself optimific. If this is so, restricted utilitarianism collapses into extreme utilitarianism. And no one could read Toulmin's book or Urmson's article on Mill without thinking that Toulmin and Urmson are of the opinion that they have thought of a doctrine which does *not* collapse into extreme utilitarianism, but which is, on the contrary, an improvement on it.

COLIN STRANG

What if Everyone
Did That?

I want to discuss the force and validity of the familiar type of
ethical argument epitomized in my title. A typical example of it
would be: "If everyone refrained from voting the result would be
disastrous, therefore *you* ought to vote." Now since the argument is
addressed to the person concerned simply *qua* member of the class
of people entitled to vote, it could be addressed with equal force
to any member or all members of that class indifferently; so the
conclusion might just as validly be: "therefore *everyone* ought to
vote."

There is no doubt that this argument has some force. People *are*
sometimes impressed by it. But it is not nearly so obvious that it is
a valid one, that is, that they *ought* to be impressed by it.

One way of not being impressed by it is to reply: "Yes, but everyone *won't* refrain from voting, so there will be no disaster, so it's
all right for me not to vote." But this reply is beside the point. The
argument never claimed that this one abstention would lead to
disaster, nor did it claim that universal abstention (which *would* be
disastrous) would occur; indeed it implied, on each point, the very
opposite. This brings out the important fact that the argument does
not appeal to the consequences of the action it condemns and so is

---

* From *Durham University Journal,* 53 (1960), 5–10. Reprinted by permission
of *Durham University Journal* and the author.

not of a utilitarian type, but that it is applicable, if anywhere, just where utilitarian arguments do *not* apply.

The objector, who remains unimpressed, will continue: "Granted that my first objection is beside the point, I still can't see how you get from your premiss to your conclusion. Your premiss is, roughly: 'Everyone's nonvoting is to be deplored,' and your conclusion is: 'Everyone's voting is obligatory.' Why should it be irrational to accept the premiss but deny the conclusion? In any case the validity of the argument cannot depend on its form alone. Plenty of arguments of the very same form are plainly invalid. For instance; if everyone switched on their electric fires at 9 a.m. sharp there would be a power breakdown, therefore no one should; furthermore, this argument applies not only to 9 a.m. but to all times, so no one should ever switch on an electric fire. Again, if everyone taught philosophy whole-time we should all starve, so no one should; or if everyone built houses or did anything else whatever (bar farming) whole-time, we should all starve; and if everyone farmed we would be without clothes or shelter and would die of exposure in winter, so no one should farm. It rather looks, on your kind of argument, as if every whole-time activity is forbidden to everyone. Conversely, if no one farmed we would all starve, so everyone should farm; if no one made clothes we would all die of exposure, so everyone ought to make clothes—and so on. So it also looks, on your kind of argument, as if all sorts of part-time activity are obligatory on everybody. You surely do not mean to commit yourself to enjoining self-sufficiency and condemning specialization? What I want to know is why some arguments of this form are valid (as you claim) while others are not (as you must admit)."

In face of this kind of objection the obvious move is to place certain restrictions on the use of arguments of this form, and to show that only those satisfying certain conditions are valid while the rest are not. This is in fact the move adopted in two recent treatments of this problem: one is by A. C. Ewing (*Philosophy*, January 1953), and the other by M. G. Singer (*Mind*, July 1955). These two are independent, since Singer makes no mention of Ewing; and Ewing, incidentally, regards himself as doing pioneer work in the subject, being able to quote only one previous treatment of it (C. D. Broad, *International Journal of Ethics*, 1915–16). But the restrictions these two wish to impose on the argument seem to me *ad hoc;* they fail to explain why the argument is valid in the remaining cases, and it is just this that I aim to discover.

Compare the voting case with this one: "If everyone here refuses to dig a latrine the camp will be insanitary, therefore everyone ought to dig one." Surely the conclusion we want is, rather: "therefore *someone* ought to dig one." In the voting case, on the other hand, given the premiss "If everyone refused to vote there would be no government," the conclusion "therefore someone ought to vote" clearly will not do; and even the conclusion "therefore everyone ought to vote" is hardly cogent on the reasonable assumption that a 10 per cent abstention will do no harm. If the argument is to be at all cogent it must make some reference to the percentage vote (say n%) needed, thus: If more than (100–n) per cent of the electorate abstained there would be no government"; this allows us to draw an acceptable conclusion, that is, "therefore n per cent must vote to avert anarchy and one must dig to avert disease. But our argument has gained in cogency and precision (being now of a simple utilitarian kind) only at the expense of being no longer effective, or even seemingly so, against the defaulter. He will reply: "All right, so n per cent ought to vote (someone ought to dig), but why me?" However, there is hope yet for the moralist. To the retort "Why me?" the argument may not suggest any obvious reply; but the retort itself does suggest the counterretort "Why not you?", to which again there is no obvious reply. An impasse is thus reached in which the moralist cannot say why the defaulter should vote or dig, and the defaulter cannot say why he should not. Evidently it was a mistake to amend the original argument, and yet there seemed to be something wrong with it as it stood; and yet, as it stood, it still seemed to be giving an answer, however obscurely, to the baffling question "Why me?": "Because if *everyone* did that . . ."

To return to the camp: certainly it is agreed by all members of the party that some digging ought to be done, and it is also agreed that the duty does not lie on anyone outside the party. But just where it lies within the party is hard to say. It does not lie on everyone, nor on anyone in particular. Where then? Whatever the answer to that apparently pressing question may be, we all know what would in fact happen. Someone would volunteer, or a leader would allot duties, or the whole party would cast lots. Or, if the thing to be done were not a once-and-for-all job like digging latrines but a daily routine like washing up, they might take it in turns.

Although various acceptable answers to the question how the duties are to be allotted are readily listed, they leave us quite in the dark as to just *who* ought to dig, wash up, and so forth. That question hardly seems to arise. In the absence of an argumentative defaulter there is no call to think up reasons why I or you should do this or that or reasons why I or you should not, and we are left with the defaulter's "Why me?" and the moralist's "Why not you?" unanswered.

Our enquiry has made little progress, but the fog is beginning to lift from the territory ahead. We are evidently concerned with communities of people and with things that must be done, or not done, if the community is to be saved from damage or destruction; and we want to know whose duty it is to do, or not to do, these things. The complexity of the problem is no longer in doubt. (1) There are some things that need doing once, some that need doing at regular intervals, and some that need doing all the time. (2) Some things need doing by one person, some by a number of people which can be roughly estimated, and some by as many as possible. (3) In practice, who shall do what (though not who *ought* to do what) is determined by economic factors, or by statutory direction (*e.g.* service with the armed forces in war, paying income tax), or merely by people's inclinations generally, that is, when enough people are inclined to do the thing anyway.

Somewhere in this territory our quarry has its lair. The following dialogue between defaulter and moralist on the evasion of income tax and military service begins the hunt. Our first steps are taken on already familiar ground:

Defaulter. £100 is a drop in the ocean to the exchequer. No one will suffer from their loss of £100, but it means a good deal to me.
Moralist. But what if everyone did that and offered the same excuse?
D. But the vast majority won't, so no one will suffer.
M. Still, would you say it was *in order* for anyone whatever to evade tax and excuse himself on the same grounds as you do?
D. Certainly.
M. So it would be quite in order for *everyone* to do the same and offer the same excuse?

D. Yes.

M. Even though disaster would ensue for the exchequer and for everyone?

D. Yes. The exchequer would no more miss my £100 if *everyone* evaded than they would if only I evaded. They wouldn't miss anyone's individual evasion. What they would miss would be the aggregate £1,000,-000,000 or so, and that isn't my default or yours or anyone's. So even if everyone evades it is still all right for me to evade; and if it's all right for me to evade it's all right for everyone to evade.

M. You seem now to be in the paradoxical position of saying that if everyone evaded it would be disastrous, and yet no one would be to blame.

D. Paradoxical, perhaps, but instructive. I am not alarmed. Let me recur to one of your previous questions: you asked whether it would be in order for all to evade and give the same excuse. I now want to reply: No, it would not be in order, but only in the sense that it would be disastrous; but it *would* be in order in the sense that each person's grounds for evasion would still be as valid as they would have been if he had been the *only* evader and no disaster had ensued. In other words, none of the defaulters would be to blame for the disaster—and certainly not one of them would blame himself: on the contrary, each one would argue that had he paid he would have been the only one to pay and thus lost his £100 without doing himself or anyone else any good. He would have been a mug to pay.

M. But surely there can't be a disaster of this kind for which no one is to blame.

D. If anyone is to blame it is the person whose job it is to circumvent evasion. If too few people vote, then it should be made illegal not to vote. If too few people volunteer, then you must introduce conscription. If too many people evade taxes, then you must tighten up your system of enforcement. My answer to your "If everyone did that" is: Then someone had jolly well better see to it that they don't; it doesn't impress me as a reason why *I* should, however many people do or don't.

M. But surely you are being inconsistent here. Take the case of evading military service.

D. You mean not volunteering in time of crisis, there being no conscription? I do that too.

M. Good. As I was saying, aren't you being inconsistent? You think *both* that it is all right not to volunteer even if too few other people volunteer (because one soldier more or less could make no difference), *and* think that you ought to be conscripted.

D. But that is not at all inconsistent. Look: the enemy threatens, a mere handful volunteer, and the writing is on the wall; my volunteering will not affect the outcome, but conscript me with the rest to stay the deluge and I will come without a murmur. In short, no good will come of my volunteering, but a great good will come of a general conscription which gathers me in with the rest. There is no inconsistency. I should add that my volunteering would in fact do positive harm: all who resist and survive are to be executed forthwith. There will be one or two heroes, but I did not think you were requiring me to be heroic.

M. I confirm that I was not, and I concede that your position is not inconsistent, however unedifying. As I see it, the nub of your position is this: Given the premiss "if everyone did that the result would be disastrous" you cannot conclude "therefore *you* oughtn't" but only "therefore someone ought to see to it that they don't." If you are right, the "if everyone did" argument, as usually taken, is invalid. But then we are left with the question: Whence does it derive its apparent force?

D. Whence, indeed?

(interval)

M. Suppose when you give your justification for evading ("no one will miss *my* contribution") I reply: But don't you think it *unfair* that other people should bear the burden which you shirk and from the bearing of which by others you derive benefit for yourself?

D. Well, yes, it is rather unfair. Indeed you make me feel a little ashamed; but I wasn't prepared, and I'm still not, to let your pet argument by without a fight. Just where does fairness come into it?

M. I think I can see. Let me begin by pushing two or three counters from different points on the periphery of the problem with the hope that they will meet at the centre. First, then: if someone is morally obliged (or permitted or forbidden) to do some particular thing, then there is a reason why he is so obliged. Further, if someone is obliged to do something for a particular reason, then anyone else whatever is equally obliged provided the reason applies to him also. The reason why a particular person is obliged to do something will be expressible in general terms, and could be expressed by describing some class to which he belongs. My principle then reads as follows: If someone is obliged to do something *just because* he is a member of a certain class, then any other member of that class will be equally obliged to do that thing. You yourself argued, remember, that any member of the class of people whose contribution would not be missed (here I allude to your reason for evasion) was no less entitled to evade than you.

D. Agreed.

M. My second counter now comes into play. "Fairness," you will agree, is a moral term like "rightness." An act is unfair if it results in someone getting a greater or lesser share of something (whether pleasant or unpleasant) than he ought to get—more or less than his fair share, as we say.

Now there are a number of things, burdensome or otherwise, which need to be done if the community is not to suffer. But who precisely is to do them? Why me? Why not me? You will also agree, I hope, to the wide principle that where the thing to be done is burdensome the burden should be fairly distributed?

D. Certainly. I seldom dispute a truism. But in what does a fair distribution consist?

M. In other words: given two people and a burden, how much of it ought each to bear? I say: *unless there is some reason why one should bear more or less of it than the other, they should both bear the same amount.* This is my Fairness Principle. It concerns both the fair allocation of the burden to some class of community members and the fair distribution of it within that class (and this may mean dividing the class into sub-classes of "isophoric" members): there must always be a *reason* for treating people differently. For instance, people who are unfit or above or below a certain age are exempted or excluded from military service, and for good reasons; women are exempted or excluded from certain kinds of military service, for what Plato regarded as bad reasons; those with more income pay more tax, while those with more children pay less, and for good reasons—and so on. You will have noticed that the typical complaint about unfair dealing begins with a "why": "Why did they charge me more than him?" (unfair distribution), or "Why should married couples be liable for so much surtax?" (unfair allocation). The maxim governing differential treatment, that is, which is behind the reasons given for it, seems to be: From each according to his resources, to each according to his need. You might argue that my principle about equal burdens is no more than a special case of this maxim. But that principle is all I need for my argument and all I insist on; I shall not stick my neck out further than necessary.

D. It is not, thus far, too dangerously exposed, I think.

M. Good. We are now ready to move a little nearer to the core of the problem. But first compare the two principles I have advanced. The first was: if a thing is obligatory and so forth for one person, then it is obligatory and so forth for anyone in the same class (*i.e.* the class relevant to the reason given). This is a license to argue from one member of a class to all its members; we will call it the Universalization Principle (U-Principle). The second, which is my Fairness Principle, is: A burden laid on a particular class is to be shared equally by all its members, unless there is reason to the contrary. This, in contrast to the first, is a license to argue from the class itself to each of its members. I take it, by the way, that these two principles are independent, that neither follows from the other.

D. Granted, granted. I am impatient to know what light all this throws on your "if everyone did" argument.

M. I am coming to that. You will remember that you used the U-Principle yourself to argue that if it's all right for you to evade it's all right for everyone else. But it was no use to me in pressing my case, and we can now see why: it argues from one to all, and there was no *one* to argue from. Nor, of course, could I argue from the consequences of your act. "Why me?" you asked, and I had then no reply. But I did at least have a retort: "Why not you?" Now it seems to me that it is just my Fairness Principle that lies behind the effectiveness of this retort, for by it you can be shown to have a duty in cases like this unless you can show that you have not. You would have to show, in the military service example, that you were not a member of the class on which the duty of military service is normally (and we will assume, fairly) regarded as lying. But you cannot show this: you cannot claim to be under age or over age or blind or lame. All you claim is that you have a certain property, the property of being one whose contribution won't be missed, which is shared by every other member of the military class; and this claim, so far from being a good reason for not volunteering, now stands revealed as no reason at all.

D. Still, you didn't dispute my point that the blame for a disaster following upon wholesale evasion lay upon those duty it was, or in whose power it lay, to prevent such evasion.

M. You certainly had a point, but I can see now that you made too much of it. I concede that the authorities failed in their duty, but then the military class as a whole failed in theirs too. The duty of both was ultimately the same, to ensure the safety of the state, just as the duty of wicket-keeper and long-stop is the same, to save byes. To confine the blame to the authorities is like saying that it's all right to burn the house down so long as it's insured or that the mere existence of a police force constitutes a general license to rob banks. As for the individual defaulter, you wanted to absolve him from all blame—a claim which seemed at once plausible and paradoxical: plausible because he was not, as you rightly pointed out, to blame for the disaster (it was not his duty to prevent that, since it was not in his power to do so); paradoxical because he was surely to blame for *something*, and we now know what for: failure to bear his share of the burden allotted to his class.

D. Maybe, but it still seems to me that if I volunteer and others don't I shall be taking on an unfair share of it, and *that* can't be fair. Then again if I don't volunteer I shall be doing less than my share, and *that* can't be fair either. Whichever I do, there's something wrong. And that can't be right.

M. There are two mistakes here. Whichever you do there's something wrong, but nothing unfair; the only wrong is people failing in their duty. Fairness is an attribute of distributions, and whether you volunteer or not neither you nor anyone else are distributing anything. Nor, for that matter, are fate or circumstances, for they are not persons. That is your first mistake. Your second is this: you talk as if the lone volunteer will necessarily do more than his fair share. He may, but he needn't. If he does, that is his own look out: *volenti non fit iniuria.*

D. It's more dangerous to fight alone than as one among many. How can he ration the danger?

M. He can surrender or run away. Look, he isn't expected to be heroic or to do, or even attempt, the impossible. If two are needed to launch and man the lifeboat, the lone volunteer can only stand and wait: *he also* serves. The least a man can do is offer and hold himself ready, though sometimes it is also the most he can do.

D. Let it be so. But I am still in trouble about one thing: suppose I grant all you say about fairness and the defaulter, I'm still not clear why you choose to make your point against him in just the mysterious way you do, that is, by fixing him with your glittering eye and beginning "If everyone did that."

M. It is a little puzzling, isn't it? But not all that puzzling. After all, the premiss states and implies a good deal: (1) It states that wholesale evasion will have such and such results; (2) it states or implies that the results will be bad; (3) it implies strongly that a duty to prevent them must lie *somewhere;* (4) it implies that the duty does not lie solely on the person addressed (otherwise a quite different kind of argument would apply); (5) it implies, rather weakly, that nevertheless the person addressed has no better excuse for doing nothing about it than anyone else has. The conclusion is then stated that he ought to do something about it. A gap remains, to be sure; but it can't be a very big one, or people wouldn't, as they sometimes do, feel the force of the argument, however obscurely. The "Why me?" retort brings out implication (4), while the "Why not you?" counterretort brings out implication (5); and we didn't really have very far to go from there.

The argument is clearly elliptical and neds filling out with some explicit reference to the Fairness Principle. I would formalize it as follows:

Unless such and such is done, undesirable consequences X will ensue;

the burden of preventing X lies upon class Y as a whole;

each member of class Y has a *prima facie* duty to bear an equal share of the burden by doing Z;

you are a member of class Y;

therefore you have a *prima facie* duty to do Z.

I have introduced the notion of a *prima facie* duty at this late stage to cover those cases where only a few members of class Y are required to do Z and it would be silly to put them all to work. In the latrine case only one person needs to dig, and in America only a small proportion of fit persons are required for short-term military service. In such cases it is considered fair to select the requisite number by lot. Until the lot is cast I must hold myself ready; if I am selected my *prima facie* duty becomes an actual duty; if I am spared, it lapses. Why selection by lot should be a fair method I leave you to work out for yourself.

Notice that the argument only holds if the thing to be done is burdensome. Voting isn't really very burdensome; indeed a lot of people seem to enjoy it, and this accounts for the weakness of the argument in this application. If the thing to be done were positively enjoyable one might even have to invoke the Fairness Principle against over-indulgence.

Notice, finally, that the argument doesn't apply unless there is a fairly readily isolable class to which a burden can be allotted. This rules out the farming and such like cases. You can't lay it down that the burden of providing food for the nation (if it *is* a burden) lies on the farmers (*i.e.* the class that provides food for the nation), for that is a tautology, or perhaps it implies the curious proposition that everyone *ought* to be doing the job he *is* doing. Might one say instead that *everyone* has a *prima facie* duty to farm, but that the duty lapses when inclination, ability and economic reward conspire to select a sufficient farming force? Far-fetched, I think. The matter might be pursued, but only at the risk of tedium. Well, are you satisfied?

D. Up to a point. Your hypothesis obviously calls for a lot more testing yet. But I have carried the burden a good deal further than my fair share of the distance; let others take it from here.

RICHARD B. BRANDT

Toward a Credible
Form of Utilitarianism

INTRODUCTION

This paper is an attempt to formulate, in a tolerably precise way, a
type of utilitarian ethical theory which is not open to obvious and
catastrophic objections. It is not my aim especially to advocate the
kind of view finally stated, although I do believe it is more acceptable than any other type of utilitarianism.

Utilitarianism is a topic discussed by contemporary moralists in
either, or both, of two contexts. One of these contexts is that of traditional normative discussion of the correct answer to such questions as "What do all right actions have in common?" Many lin-
guistically oriented philosophers do not believe such questions are
a proper subject for philosophical discussion, but noncognitivists
in metaethics can, as well as anyone else, consistently defend (or
criticize) a utilitarian normative ethic, not claiming that such a
theory is strictly true but nevertheless offering arguments of a kind.

Utilitarianism also plays a substantial part in contemporary metaethical discussions. If you ask some philosophers what can count as
a good or valid reason for an ethical judgment, you may be told
that some kind of utilitarian reason—inference from good conse-

* Reprinted from *Morality and the Language of Conduct*, by Hector-Neri
Castaneda and George Nakhnikian, by permission of the Wayne State University
Press and the author. Copyright 1963 by the Wayne State University Press.

quences to rightness—is one kind, or even the only kind. This view may be supported by urgings that this is the kind of reasoning people actually do use, or by saying that this is the kind of reasoning used in reflective moments by people whom we should count as reliable moral judges. Alternatively, it may be argued that this kind of reasoning is the kind that should be used—regardless of whether it is used—in view of the function of ethical reasoning and conscience in society, or in view of what counts as a "moral judgment" or as "moral reasoning" or as "justified ethical reasoning."

Discussions of utilitarianism in these two contexts are not as different as might at first appear. If some kind of utilitarian reasoning can be shown to be what reflective people do use, or if it can be shown to be the kind all ought to use, then presumably utilitarianism as a normative position—as the one "valid" principle in normative ethics—can be established, in the way we can expect to establish such things in ethics.

The formulation of utilitarianism I shall work out in this paper, then, can be viewed in either of two ways, corresponding with the persuasions of the reader. It can be viewed as a candidate for the status of normative "truth," or, for the noncognitivist, for whatever status is in his theory the analogue of truth in cognitivist theories. Or it can be viewed as a way of thinking or reasoning, as a rule of valid inference—the central theme either of considerations which play a role in the ethical inferences of reliable moral judges, or of considerations which would play a certain role in ethical thinking if we thought as we ought to do, in view of the functions (*etc.*) of ethical discourse. One way of putting the contrast is this: we can view our formulation either as a candidate for the status of being a true principle of normative ethics or as a rule for valid inferences in ethics. I am not, incidentally, suggesting that it is a merely terminological matter which view we take of it; I think it is *not* merely this, since the kinds of reasoning used to support one view may be quite different from those used to support the other view. My point is that the theory I wish to discuss may properly be considered in either light, and that the difficulties I shall raise are difficulties which must be taken seriously by philosophers who discuss utilitarianism in either of these contexts. Mostly, I shall talk for convenience as if utilitarianism were a normative principle; but everything I say, and all the difficulties I consider, can just as well be placed in the context of metaethical discussion.

The view to be discussed is a form of "rule-utilitarianism." This terminology must be explained. I call a utilitarianism "act-utilitarianism" if it holds that the rightness of an act is fixed by the utility of *its* consequences, as compared with those of other acts the agent might perform instead. Act-utilitarianism is hence an atomistic theory: the value of the effects of a single act on the world is decisive for its rightness. "Rule-utilitarianism," in contrast, applies to views according to which the rightness of an act is not fixed by *its* relative utility, but by conformity with general rules or principles; the utilitarian feature of these theories consists in the fact that the correctness of these rules or principles is fixed in some way by the utility of their general acceptance. In contrast with the atomism of act-utilitarianism, rule-utilitarianism is in a sense an organic theory: the rightness of individual acts can be ascertained only by assessing a whole social policy.

Neither form of utilitarianism is necessarily committed on the subject of what counts as "utility": not on the meaning or function of such phrases as "maximize intrinsic good," and not on the identity of intrinsic goods—whether enjoyments, or states of persons, or states of affairs, such as equality of distribution.

In recent years, types of rule-utilitarianism have been the object of much interest.[1] And for good reason. Act-utilitarianism, at least given the assumptions about what is valuable which utilitarians commonly make, has implications which it is difficult to accept.[2] It

[1] In one form or another its plausibility has been urged by J. O. Urmson, Kurt Baier, J. D. Mabbott, Stephen Toulmin, R. F. Harrod, Kai Neilsen, A. MacBeath, C. A. Campbell, Jonathan Harrison, Marcus Singer, and, to some extent, John Rawls and P. H. Nowell-Smith. Mabbott has expressed the opinion that the essence of it is to be found in Francis Hutcheson.

[2] In this paper I propose to ignore that form of act-utilitarianism which proposes to close the gap between what seems to be right and the implications of act-utilitarianism, by asserting that such things as promise-keeping are intrinsically good. This form of theory has most recently been defended by Oliver Johnson in his *Rightness and Goodness* (The Hague: Martinus Nijhoff, 1959).

I am inclined to agree that there are some intrinsically good things which are not states of persons—for instance, equality of distribution of welfare. But act-utilitarians require to count further things—such as specific traits of character like truthfulness, or complexes like the-keeping-of-a-promise—as intrinsically

implies that if you have employed a boy to mow your lawn and he has finished the job and asks for his pay, you should pay him what you promised only if you cannot find a better use for your money. It implies that when you bring home your monthly pay-check you should use it to support your family and yourself only if it cannot be used more effectively to supply the needs of others. It implies that if your father is ill and has no prospect of good in his life, and maintaining him is a drain on the energy and enjoyments of others, then, if you can end his life without provoking any public scandal or setting a bad example, it is your positive duty to take matters into your own hands and bring his life to a close. A virtue of rule-utilitarianism, in at least some of its forms, is that it avoids at least some of such objectionable implications.

In the present paper I wish to arrive at a more precise formulation of a rule-utilitarian type of theory which is different from act-utilitarianism and which is not subject to obvious and catastrophic difficulties. To this end I shall, after an important preliminary discussion, begin by considering two formulations, both supported by distinguished philosophers, which, as I shall show, lead us in the wrong direction. This discussion will lead to a new formulation devised to avoid the consequences of the first theories. I shall then

---

good in order to square with reasonable convictions about what is right or wrong. But surely it is contrary to the spirit of utilitarianism to decide the issue, say, whether a promise should be kept by appeal to such intrinsic values. One would have thought the utilitarian would test the merits of traits of character like truthfulness by examining whether they have good consequences rather than decide that there is an obligation to tell the truth by considering the intrinsic goodness of truthfulness. Should not the issue of the intrinsic goodness of truthfulness wait upon reasoning to show that it is a good thing to tell the truth? One who denies this is far from traditional utilitarian thought. In any case, can we seriously claim that the-keeping-of-a-promise is an intrinsic good? It would be absurd to hold that we can add to the value of the world by the simple device of making promises and then keeping them, irrespective of what is effected by the keeping of them. Presumably, then, what is held is rather that the-breaking-of-a-promise is intrinsically bad. But how will it be shown that precisely this is intrinsically bad? Suppose I promise to do something no one wants done, and everyone is greatly relieved when I fail to perform. Is this intrinsically evil?

The kind of utilitarianism I propose here to discuss is one with narrower commitments about what is intrinsically good—one which does not claim that specific kinds of action or specific traits of character (like truthfulness or fidelity) are intrinsically good or bad. This kind of utilitarianism is worth assessment even if my reasons for ignoring other types are unsound.

describe three problems which the new theory seems to face, and consider how—by amendments or otherwise—these difficulties may be met.

1. UTILITARIANISM AS A THEORY ABOUT THE OBJECTIVELY RIGHT

Before we can proceed there is a preliminary issue to be settled. It is generally agreed that utilitarianism is a proposal about which acts are *right* or *wrong*. Unfortunately it is also widely held—although this is a matter of dispute—that these terms are used in several senses. Hence, in order to state the utilitarian thesis clearly, we must identify which sense of these words (if there is more than one) we have in mind. Utilitarianism may be clearly false in all of its forms if it is construed as a universal statement about which acts are right or wrong, in some of the senses in which these words are, or at least are supposed to be, used.

It is plausible to say that "wrong" is sometimes used in a sense equivalent to "morally blameworthy" or "reprehensible," in a sense which implies the propriety of disapproval of the agent for his deed. Now, if utilitarianism is understood as a theory about right and wrong actions in this sense, I believe it is an indefensible theory in all its forms. For we have good reason to think that whether an act is wrong in this sense depends in part on such things as whether the agent sincerely believed he was doing his duty, whether the temptation to do what he did was so strong that only a person of very unusual firmness of will would have succeeded in withstanding it, and whether the agent's action was impulsive and provoked, or deliberate and unprovoked. If whether an act is wrong depends in part on any one of these factors, then it is difficult to see how the utilitarian thesis that rightness or wrongness is in some sense a function of utility can be correct.

We can, however, construe utilitarianism as a thesis about which acts are right or wrong in some other sense. It may, for instance, be taken as a theory about which acts are right or wrong in a forward-looking sense, which I shall call the "objective" sense. But what is this sense? It is by no means easy to say; and we must be careful not to describe some alleged sense of these words which in fact they never bear in common speech at all. Let me explain this possible second sense by means of an example.

Consider Eisenhower's position at the summit conference in 1960. Khrushchev demanded that Eisenhower apologize, as a condition for negotiation. Let us suppose that Eisenhower proceeded to ask himself the moral question, "What is the morally right thing for me to do now? Is it my moral obligation to apologize or to refuse to apologize?" Clearly, it would seem, this is a question he might have asked himself, whether he did or not. Obviously, if he did try to answer this question, he must have considered many things. One thing he must have considered was the state of Khrushchev's mind. Did Khrushchev really think there had been a breach of faith, an affront to the Russian people, which in decency called for at least an apology? Was Khrushchev really willing to negotiate for peace if only this—which might relieve some political pressures at home— were done? Everything considered, would an apology, however personally distasteful (and perhaps politically unfortunate, at home), markedly promote the cause of peace? Let us suppose that Eisenhower surveyed these points as carefully as possible with his advisers and came to a conclusion on them. And let us suppose that he then moved to a moral conclusion. Presumably his conclusion (if he raised the moral question) was that it was not his duty to apologize, that on the contrary it was his duty *not* to apologize. But surely in a complex situation of this sort he must have put his conclusion in a qualified way; he must have said something like, "*Probably* it is my duty not to apologize." And, conceivably, he might some day change his mind about this, and say to himself, "It was my duty to apologize; my judgment then was mistaken." I think we shall all agree that he might well have expressed himself in this qualified way and that he might later revise his judgment in the manner suggested.

The crucial thing about understanding the sense in which "duty" (or "wrong") is here being used is whether the qualifying "probably" is introduced or whether the revision conceding a "mistake" may be made, for one reason or for another. Does he say "probably" because he does not and cannot know Khrushchev's real state of mind? Does he say a "mistake" was made because, as it turns out, Khrushchev's state of mind was really different from what at the time he supposed it to be? If the answer to these questions is affirmative, then evidently duty depends, at least to some extent, on what the facts really are and not merely on what one thinks they are, even after careful consultation with advisers. But if the answer is negative, then it is open to one to say that the qualification and mistakes come in only because it is so difficult to *balance* different considerations, and that what is one's duty does not depend on what the facts really are, but only on what one thinks they are, at least after properly careful reflection and investigation.

If we answer these questions in the affirmative and consequently say that "duty" is sometimes used in a sense such that whether something is one's duty depends on what the facts really are, then we are conceding that the word (and, presumably, "right" and "wrong" and "moral obligations") is sometimes used in an "objective" sense— the sense in which G. E. Moore thought it was sometimes used when he wrote *Ethics* and *Principia Ethica*. And if so, it is not entirely stupid to propose, as Moore did, that furthermore, an act is right, in that objective sense of "right," if and only if its *actual* consequences, whether foreseeable at the time or not, are such that the performance of the act produces at least as much intrinsic good as could be produced by any other act the agent could perform instead. It is this sense of these terms—the sense in which duty (*etc.*) depends on what the facts really are and not on what the agent thinks about them—which I am terming the "objective" sense. I shall construe utilitarianism as a proposal about which acts are right or wrong in this objective sense.

It would be foolish, however, to say that it is quite *obvious* that the answer to the above questions is in the affirmative; and consequently it would be foolish to affirm without doubt that there is a sense of "duty" in which duty depends on what the facts are and not on what the agent thinks they are—and much more foolish to affirm without doubt that there is *no* sense of "duty" in which duty depends, not on the facts, but on what the agent thinks the facts are, at least after properly careful investigation.

Philosophers who think these words have no "objective" sense at all, or who at least think there is still a third sense of these terms, over and above the two I have sketched, probably can mostly be said to think that these words are used in what we may call the "subjective" sense—and either that this is their only sense or that it is one ordinary sense. They do not agree among themselves about what this sense is. Some of them hold that "right" (etc.) is sometimes so used that—if I may identify their conception by my own terminology, which, of course, some of them would not accept—an act is right in that sense if and only if it would have been right in my objective sense, if the facts had really been what the agent thought they were, or at least would have thought they were if he had investigated properly. What is one's duty, on this view, depends on what the agent thinks about the facts—or would think if he investigated properly—not on what the facts really are. Naturally, if one has this (alleged) sense of "duty" or "right" in mind when formulating the principle of utilitarianism, one will say the principle is that an act is right if and only if the agent *thinks*—or would think, if he investigated properly—it will maximize utility (or have some such relation to utility). Or, perhaps, the principle will say that an act is right if and only if it will maximize expectable utility, or something of the sort.

The question whether there is an objective sense, or a subjective sense, or perhaps both such senses, is a difficult one. Although I think it plausible to suppose there is an "objective" sense, I do feel doubt about the matter. I propose, nevertheless, to discuss utilitarianism as a theory about right and wrong in this sense. I do so for several reasons. First, there are many philosophers who think there is such a sense, and an examination of utilitarianism construed in this way "speaks to their condition." [3] Second, even if there were no such ordinary sense of "right," we could define such a sense by reference to the "subjective" sense of "right" (assuming there is one); and it so happens that we could say all the things that we have occasion to say in ethics by using this defined "objective" sense of "right" and also terms like "blameworthy" and "reprehensible." We could say

[3] Notice that such philosophers are not refuted by the mere consideration that sometimes we say "is right" and not "is probably right" even when we know we lack evidence about some facts that might be relevant to what is right in the objective sense. It would be a mistake to infer from such usage that we are not employing "right" in the objective sense. For, in general, we are entitled to make any assertion roundly without the qualifying word "probable" if we know of no definite grounds for questioning the truth of the assertion.

"all we have occasion to say" in the sense that any statement we make, and think important, could be put in terms of this vocabulary. Third, it is important to see how types of rule-utilitarian theory fare if they are construed as theories about which acts are right or wrong in this sense. Doubtless sometimes writers on this topic have not kept clearly in mind just which sense of "right" they were talking about; it is useful to see what difficulties arise *if* they are to be taken as talking of what is right or wrong in the objective sense. Finally, an assessment of utilitarianisms as theories about which acts are objectively right will enable us to make at least some assessments of utilitarianisms as theories about which acts are subjectively right, in view of the logical connection indicated above between "right" in the objective sense and "right" in the subjective sense.

2. ACCEPTED RULES VS. JUSTIFIABLE RULES AS THE TEST OF RIGHTNESS

It is convenient to begin by taking as our text some statements drawn from an interesting article by J. O. Urmson. In this paper, Urmson suggested that John Stuart Mill should be interpreted as a rule-utilitarian; and Urmson's opinion was that Mill's view would be more plausible if he were so interpreted. Urmson summarized the possible rule-utilitarian interpretation of Mill in four propositions, of which I quote the first two:

A. A particular action is justified as being right [in the sense of being morally obligatory] by showing that it is in accord with [is required by] some moral rule. It is shown to be wrong by showing that it transgresses some moral rule.

B. A moral rule is shown to be correct by showing that the recognition of that rule promotes the ultimate end.[4]

Urmson's first proposition could be taken in either of two ways. When it speaks of a "moral rule," it may refer to an *accepted* moral rule, presumably one accepted in the society of the agent. Alternatively, it may refer to a *correct* moral rule, presumably one the recognition of which promotes the ultimate end. If we ask in which way the proposed theory should be taken, in order to arrive at a

---

[4] J. O. Urmson, "The Interpretation of the Philosophy of J. S. Mill," *Philosophical Quarterly*, III (1953), 33–39.

defensible theory, part of the answer is that qualifications are going to be required, whichever way we take it. I think it more worthwhile and promising, however, to try to develop it in the second interpretation.

Various philosophers would make the opposite judgment about which interpretation is the more promising. And there is much to be said for their view, in particular the following points. First, we shall probably all agree that the moral rules accepted in a community often do fix real obligations on members of the community. For example, among ourselves it is taken for granted that primary responsibility for caring for an old man falls on his children, although in special cases it could fall elsewhere. On the other hand, suppose that our social system contained the rule—as that of the Hopi actually does—that this responsibility falls primarily on the children of a man's sisters, again with exceptions for special cases. It seems clear that in a social system like ours the children do have responsibility for their father, whereas in a social system like that of the Hopi they do not—the responsibility belongs to the children of the sisters. There are complications, to be sure; but in general we must say that when an institutional system specifies that responsibility falls in a certain place, then on the whole and with some exceptions and qualifications, that is where it really does lie. Any theory which denies this is mistaken; and if our second theory is to be plausible, it must be framed so as to imply this. Second, I think we should concede that if two persons are debating whether some act is right and one of them is able to show that it infringes on the accepted moral code of the community, the "burden of proof" passes to the other party. The fact that it is generally believed that a certain kind of action is wrong is *prima facie* evidence that it is wrong; it is up to persons who disagree to show their hand. Third, if a conscientious man is deliberating whether he is morally obligated to do a certain thing which he does not wish to do, I believe he will generally feel he must do this thing, even if he thinks that a correct moral code would not require him to, provided he concludes that many or most persons in his community would conclude otherwise. The reason for this is partly, I think, that a conscientious man will take pains to avoid even the appearance of evil; but the reason is also that a conscientious man will wish to make substantial allowances for the fact that he is an interested party and might have been influenced by his own preferences in his thinking about his obligations. He will therefore tend to hold himself to the received code when this is to his disadvantage.

Nevertheless, it is extremely difficult to defend Urmson's rule interpreted in this way, even when we hedge it with qualifications, as, for example, Toulmin did. In the first place, people do not *think* that anything like this is true; they think they are assessing particular cases by reference to objectively valid principles which they happen to know, and not simply by reference to a community code. Notice how we do not find it surprising that people with unusual moral principles, such as the immorality of killing and violence in all circumstances, come to distinctive conclusions about their own particular obligations, by no means drawing their particular moral judgments from the code of the community. The whole tradition emphasizing the role of conscience in moral thinking is contrary to the view that socially accepted principles are crucial for deciding what is right or wrong. In the second place, we frequently judge ourselves to have moral obligations either when we don't know what the community "standards" are, or when we think that in all probability there is no decided majority one way or the other: for instance, with respect to sexual behavior, or to declaration, to revenue officers, of articles purchased abroad or of one's personal income. Surely we do not think that in such situations the proper judgment of particular cases is that they are morally indifferent? Third, and perhaps most important, we sometimes judge that we have an obligation when we know that the community thinks we don't; and we sometimes think an act is right when the community thinks it wrong. For instance, we may judge that we have an obligation to join in seeking presidential clemency for a convicted Communist spy whom we regard as having received an unduly severe sentence because of mass hysteria at the time of his trial, although we know quite well that the communal code prescribes no favors for Communists. Again, we may think it not wrong to work on the Sabbath, marry a divorced person, perform a medically necessary abortion, or commit suicide, irrespective of general disapproval in our group. Were these things *ever* objectively wrong, in view of being proscribed—even unanimously—by the community of the agent? (It may be replied that the "code" does not legislate for complex matters of these sorts, but only for more basic things, like Ross's list of *prima facie* obligations. But it is not clear what can be the basis for this distinction; the acts in question may be prohibited by law and would be reported by a visiting anthropologist as proscribed by the code.)

One might argue that the existence of an accepted moral rule is not sufficient to make particular actions wrong or obligatory but is a necessary condition. To say this, however, is to say that men have no obligation to rise above the commonplace morals of their times. Whereas in fact we do not think it right for men to be cruel to animals or to slaves in a society which condones this.

We cannot well say in advance that no thesis like Urmson's can play an important part in a defensible theory of morals, if it is interpreted in this first way. But the difficulties are surely enough to encourage experimenting with versions of the second interpretation. Let us turn to this.

For a start, we might summarize the gist of Urmson's proposal, construed in the second way, as follows: "An act is right if and only if it conforms with that set of moral rules, the recognition of which would have significantly desirable consequences." A somewhat modified version of this is what I shall be urging.

One minor amendment I wish to make immediately. I think we should replace the second clause by the expression, "the recognition of which would have the *best* consequences." This amendment may be criticized on the ground that the business of moral rules is with commanding or prohibiting actions whose performance or omission would be quite harmful if practiced widely, but not to require actions which just maximize benefits, especially if the benefit concerns only the agent. It may be said, then, that the amendment I propose is possibly a clue to *perfect* behavior but not to right behavior. But this objection overlooks an important point. We must remember that it is a serious matter to have a moral rule at all, for moral rules take conduct out of the realm of preference and free decision. So, for the recognition of a certain moral rule to have good consequences, the benefits of recognition must outweigh the costliness of restricting freedom. Therefore, to recognize a moral rule restricting self-regarding behavior will rarely have the best consequences; rules of prudence should normally not be moral rules. Again, my proposal implies that moral rules will require services for other people only when it is better to have such services performed from a sense of obligation than not performed at all; so the amendment does not commit us to saying that it is morally obligatory to perform minor altruistic services for others.

But why insist on the amendment? The reason is that the original, as I stated it (but not necessarily as Urmson intended it), is insufficiently comparative in form. The implication is that a rule is acceptable so long as it is significantly better than no regulation at all. But the effect of this is tolerantly to accept a great many rules which we should hardly regard as morally acceptable. Consider promises. There are various possible rules about when promises must be kept. One such possible rule is to require keeping *all* promises, absolutely irrespective of unforeseeable and uncontemplated hardships on the promisee. Recognition of this rule might have good consequences as compared with no rule at all. Therefore it seems to satisfy the unamended formula. Many similar rules would satisfy it. But we know of another rule—the one we recognize—with specifications about allowable exceptions, which would have much better consequences. If we are utilitarian in spirit, we shall want to endorse such a rule but not both of these rules; and the second one is much closer to our view about what our obligations are. The amendment in general endorses as correct many rules which command our support for parallel reasons, and refuses to endorse many others which we reject for parallel reasons.

3. A SPECIOUS RULE-UTILITARIANISM

I shall now digress briefly, in order to bring out the importance of avoiding a form of rule-utilitarianism which seems to differ only insignificantly from our above initial suggestion, and which at first seems most attractive. It is worthwhile doing so, partly because two very interesting and important papers developing a rule-utilitarian theory may be construed as falling into the trap I shall describe.[5] I

[5] These articles are: J. Harrison, "Utilitarianism, Universalization, and Our Duty to be Just," *Proceedings of the Aristotelian Society*, Vol. LIII (1952–53), pp. 105–34; and R. F. Harrod, "Utilitarianism Revised," *Mind*, n.s. XLV (1936), 137–56.

say only that they "may be" so construed because their authors are possibly using somewhat different concepts and, in particular, may not be thinking of utilitarianism as a thesis about right and wrong in the objective sense.

Suppose that we wrote, instead of the above suggested formulation, the following: "An act is right if and only if it conforms with that set of moral rules, general conformity with which would have best consequences." This phrasing is a bit vague, however, so let us expand it to this: "An act is right if and only if it conforms with that set of general prescriptions for action such that, if everyone always did, from among all the things which he could do on a given occasion, what conformed with these prescriptions, then at least as much intrinsic good would be produced as by conformity with any other set of general prescriptions." This sounds very like our above formulation. It is, however, different in a very important way: for its test of whether an act is right, or a general rule correct, is what would happen if people *really all did act* in a certain way. The test is not the consequences of recognizing a rule, or of acting with such a rule in mind; the test as stated does not require that people do, or even can, think of or formulate, much less apply the rule of a moral code. What is being said is simply that a rule is correct, and corresponding conduct right, if it would have best consequences for everyone actually to act, for whatever reason, in accordance with the rule. Of course, one of the consequences to be taken into account may be the fact that expectations of conduct according to the rule might be built up, and that people could count on conforming behavior.

This theory is initially attractive. We seem to be appealing to it in our moral reasoning when we say, "You oughtn't to do so-and-so, because if everybody in your circumstances did this, the consequences would be bad."

Nevertheless, the fact is that this theory—however hard it may be to see that it does—has identically the same consequences for behavior as does act-utilitarianism. And since it does, it is a mistake to advocate it as a theory preferable to act-utilitarianism, as some philosophers may have done. Let us see how this is.

Let us ask ourselves: What would a set of moral prescriptions be like, such that general conformity with it, in the sense intended, would have the best consequences? The answer is that the set would contain just one rule, the prescription of the *act-utilitarian:* "Perform an act, among those open to you, which will have at least as good consequences as any other." There cannot be a moral rule, conformity with which could have better consequences than this one. If it really is true that doing a certain thing will have the very best consequences in the long run, everything considered, of all the things I can do, then there is nothing better I can do than this. If everyone always did the very best thing it was possible for him to do, the total intrinsic value produced would be at a maximum. Any act which deviated from this principle would produce less good than some other act which might have been performed. It is clear, then, that the moral rule general conformity with which would produce most good is a rule corresponding to the principle of act-utilitarianism. The two theories, then, have identical consequences for behavior. I am, of course, not at all suggesting that everyone *trying* to produce the best consequences will have the same consequences as everyone *trying* to follow some different set of rules—or that everyone trying to follow some different set of rules may not have better consequences than everyone trying just to produce the best consequences. Far from it. What I am saying is that *succeeding* in producing the best consequences is a kind of success which cannot be improved upon. And it is this which is in question, when we are examining the formula we are now looking at.

To say that succeeding in producing the best consequences cannot be improved upon is consistent with admitting that what will in fact have the best consequences, in view of what other people in fact have done or will do, may be different from what would have had the best consequences if other people were to behave differently from the way in which they did or will do. The behavior of others is part of the context relevant for determining the effects of a given act of any agent.

It may be thought that this reasoning is unfair to this rule-utilitarian view. For what this theory has in mind, it may be said, is rules forbidding classes of actions described in ways other than by reference to their utility—rules forbidding actions like lies, adultery, theft, and so forth. So, it may be said, the principle of act-utilitarianism is not even a competitor for the position of one of the rules admitted by this theory.

My reply to this objection is twofold. In the first place, it would be rather foolish to suppose that any system of moral rules could omit rules about doing good, rules about doing what will maximize utility. Surely we do wish to include among our rules one roughly to the effect that, if we have the opportunity to do a great deal of good for others at little cost, we should do it. And also a rule to the effect that we should avoid harming others. It is no accident that W. D. Ross's list of seven *prima facie* obligations contains four which refer to doing good, in one way or another. But the point would still stand even if we ignore this fact. For suppose we set about to describe a set of rules, none of which is explicitly to prescribe *doing good,* but general conformity with which will maximize utility. Now obviously, the set of rules in question will be that set which prescribes, by descriptions which make no reference to having good consequences, exactly that very class of actions which would also be prescribed by the act-utilitarian principle. And one can find a set of rules which will prescribe exactly this class of acts without referring to utility. We can find such a set, because every member of the class of acts prescribed by the act-utilitarian principle will have some other property *on account of which* it will maximize utility in the circumstances. Every act, that is to say, which maximizes utility does so because of some doubtless very complex property that it has. As a result, we can set up a system of prescriptions for action which refer to these complex properties, such that our system of rules will prescribe exactly the set of acts prescribed by the act-utilitarian principle. The set of rules may be enormously long and enormously complex. But this set of rules will have the property of being that set, general conformity with which will maximize utility. And the acts prescribed will be identical with the acts prescribed by the act-utilitarian principle. So, again, the prescriptions for conduct of this form of rule-utilitarianism are identical with those of the act-utilitarian theory.

4. RULE-UTILITARIANISM: A SECOND APPOXIMATION

The whole point of the preceding remarks has been to focus attention on the point that a rule-utilitarianism like Urmson's is different from act-utilitarianism only when it speaks of something like *"recognition* of a rule having the best consequences" instead of something like *"conformity* with a certain rule having the best consequences." With this in mind, we can see clearly one of the virtues of Urmson's proposal, which we interpreted as being: "An act is right if and only if it conforms with that set of moral rules, *the recognition of which* would have the best consequences."

But, having viewed the difficulties of a view verbally very similar to the above, we are now alert to the fact that the formulation we have suggested is itself open to interpretations that may lead to problems. How may we construe Urmson's proposal, so that it is both unambiguous and credible? Of course we do not wish to go to the opposite extreme and take "recognition of" to mean merely "doffing the hat to" without attempt to practice. But how shall we take it?

I suggest the following as a second approximation.

First, let us speak of a set of moral rules as being "learnable" if people of ordinary intelligence are able to learn or absorb its provisions, so as to believe the moral propositions in question in the ordinary sense of "believe" for such contexts.[6] Next, let us speak of "the adoption" of a moral code by a person as meaning "the learning and belief of its provisions (in the above sense) and conformity of behavior to these to the extent we may expect people of ordinary conscientiousness to conform their behavior to rules they believe are principles about right or obligatory behavior." Finally, let us, purely arbitrarily and for the sake of brevity, use the phrase "maximizes intrinsic value" to mean "would produce at least as much intrinsic good as would be produced by any relevant al-

---

[6] To say that a moral code can be learned by a person is not to say he can learn to *recite* it. It is enough if he learns it well enough to recall the relevant rule when stimulated by being in a context to which it is relevant. Learning a moral code is thus like learning a complex route into a large city: we may not be able to draw it or explain to others what it is, but when we drive it and have the landmarks before us, we remember each turn we are to make.

ternative action." With these stipulations, we can now propose, as a somewhat more precise formulation of Urmson's proposal, the following rule-utilitarian thesis: "An act is right if and only if it conforms with that learnable set of rules, the adoption of which by everyone would maximize intrinsic value."

This principle does not at all imply that the rightness or wrongness of an act is contingent upon the agent's having *thought about* all the complex business of the identity of a set of ideal moral rules; it asserts, rather, that an act is right if and only if it *conforms* to such a set of rules, regardless of what the agent may think. Therefore the principle is not disqualified from being a correct principle about what is objectively right or wrong, in Moore's sense; for it makes rightness and wrongness a matter of the facts, and totally independent of what the agent thinks is right, or of what the agent thinks about the facts, or of the evidence the agent may have, or of what is probably the case on the basis of this evidence.

An obvious merit of this principle is that it gives expression to at least part of our practice or procedure in trying to find out what is right or wrong. For when we are in doubt about such matters, we often try to think out how it would work in practice to have a moral code which prohibited or permitted various actions we are considering. We do not, of course, ordinarily do anything as complicated as try to think out the *complete* ideal moral code; we are content with considering whether certain specific injunctions relevant to the problem we are considering might be included in a good and workable code. Nevertheless, we are prepared to admit that the whole ideal code is relevant. For if someone shows us that a specific injunction which we think would be an acceptable part of a moral code clearly would not work out in view of other provisions necessary to an ideal code, we should agree that a telling point had been made and revise our thinking accordingly.

In order to get a clearer idea of the kind of "set of rules" (with which right actions must conform) which could satisfy the conditions this rule-utilitarian principle lays down, let us note some general features such a set presumably would have. First, it would contain rules giving directions for recurrent situations which involve conflicts of human interests. Presumably, then, it would contain rules rather similar to W. D. Ross's list of *prima facie* obligations:

rules about the keeping of promises and contracts, rules about debts of gratitude such as we may owe to our parents, and, of course, rules about not injuring other persons and about promoting the welfare of others where this does not work a comparable hardship on us. Second, such a set of rules would not include petty restrictions; nor, at least for the most part, would it contain purely prudential rules. Third, the rules would not be very numerous; an upper limit on quantity is set by the ability of ordinary people to learn them. Fourth, such a set of rules would not include unbearable demands; for their inclusion would only serve to bring moral obligation into discredit. Fifth, the set of rules adoption of which would have the best consequences could not leave too much to discretion. It would make concessions to the fact that ordinary people are not capable of perfectly fine discriminations, and to the fact that, not being morally perfect, people of ordinary conscientiousness will have a tendency to abuse a moral rule where it suits their interest. We must remember that a college dormitory rule like "Don't play music at such times or in such a way as to disturb the study or sleep of others" would be ideally flexible if people were perfect; since they aren't, we have to settle for a rule like "No music after 10 p.m." The same thing is true for a moral code. The best moral code has to allow for the fact that people are what they are; it has to be less flexible and less efficient than a moral code that was to be adopted by perfectly wise and perfectly conscientious people could be.

Should we think of such a moral code as containing only prescriptions for situations likely to arise in *everyone's* life—rules like "If you have made a promise, then . . ." or "If you have a parent living, then treat him thus-and-so"? Or should we think of it as containing distinct sets of prescriptions for *different roles or statuses*, such as "If you are a policeman, then . . ." or "If you are a physician, then . . ."? And if the ideal code is to contain different prescriptions for different roles and statuses, would it not be so complex that it could not be learned by people of ordinary intelligence? The answer to these questions is that the rule-utilitarian is not committed, by his theory, to the necessity of such special codes, although I believe he may well admit their desirability—admit, for instance, that it is a good thing for a physician to carry a rule in his mental kit, specially designed to answer the question, "Shall I treat a patient who does not pay his bill?" In any case, our rule-utilitarian theory can *allow* for such special rules. Nor is there a difficulty in the fact that people of normal intelligence could hardly learn all these special sets of rules. For we can mean, by saying that a code can be "learned" by people of ordinary intelligence, that any person can learn all the rules relevant to the problems *he* will face. A rule-utilitarian will not, of course, have in mind a moral code which in some part is secret—for instance, lawyers having a moral code known only to themselves, a code which it would be harmful for others to know about. For surely in the long run it could not have best consequences for a society to have a moral code, perhaps granting special privileges to some groups, which could not stand the light of public knowledge.

5. FIRST PROBLEM: MORAL CODES FOR AN IMPERFECT SOCIETY

Our "second approximation" to a rule-utilitarian principle has proposed that an act is right if and only if it conforms with the requirements of a learnable moral code, the adoption of which by *everyone* would maximize utility—and meaning by "adoption of a code" the learning and belief that the code lays down the requirements for moral behavior, and conformity to it to the extent we may expect from people of *ordinary conscientiousness*.

The italicized words in the preceding paragraph indicate two respects in which the proposed test of rightness in a sense departs from reality. In actuality moral codes are not subscribed to by everybody in all particulars: there is virtual unanimity on some items of what we call "the code of the community" (such as the prohibition of murder and incest), but on other matters there is less unanimity (in the United States, the "code" permits artificial birth-control measures despite disapproval by many Catholics), and it is a somewhat arbitrary matter to decide when the disagreement has become so general that we ought not to speak of something as part of the code of the community at all. There is probably some measure of disagreement on many or most moral matters in most modern communities (and, surely, in at least many primitive communities).

Furthermore, our proposal, in an effort to be definite about the degree of commitment involved in the "adoption" of a code, spoke of an "ordinary conscientiousness." This again departs from reality. Ordinary conscientiousness may be the exception: many people are extremely, perhaps even overly conscientious; at the other extreme, some people act as if they have developed no such thing as a conscience at all. It is characteristic of actual communities that there is a wide range in degrees of conscientiousness.

As a result of these departures from reality, our test for rightness savors a bit of the utopian. We are invited to think of different worlds, each populated by people of "ordinary conscientiousness," all of whom are inoculated with a standard moral code. We are to decide whether given types of action are right or wrong by considering which of these hypothetical communities would realize a maximum of value.

There is force in the proposal. In fact, if we are thinking of sponsoring some ideal, this conception is a useful one for appraising whatever ideal we are considering. Just as we might ask whether large military establishments or a capitalist economy would be suitable for the ideal community of the future, so we can ask whether certain features of our present moral code would be suitable in such a community. It may be that such a conception should play a large role in deciding what ultimate ideals we should espouse.

Nevertheless, this conception may, from its very framework, necessarily be unsuitable for deciding the rightness of actions in the real world. It appears that, in fact, this is the case with both of the features mentioned above.

First, the proposal is to test rightness by the desirability of a rule in a moral code among people of ordinary conscientiousness. Now, in a community composed of people of ordinary conscientiousness we do not have to provide for the contingency of either saints or great sinners. In particular, we do not have to provide for the occurrence of people like Adolf Hitler. In such a community, presumably, we could get along with a minimal police force, perhaps an unarmed police force. Similarly, it would seem there would be no value in a moral prescription like "Resist evil men." In the community envisaged, problems of a certain sort would presumably not arise, and therefore the moral code need not have features designed to meet those problems. Very likely, for instance, a moral code near to that of extreme pacifism would work at least as well as a code differing in its nonpacifism.

More serious is the flaw in the other feature: that the test of rightness is to be compatibility with the requirements of the moral code, adoption of which *by everyone* would maximize utility. The trouble with this is that it permits behavior which really would be desirable if everyone agreed, but which might be objectionable and undesirable if not everyone agreed. For instance, it may well be that it would have the best consequences if the children are regarded as responsible for an elderly parent who is ill or needy; but it would be most unfortunate if the members of a Hopi man's native household—primarily his sisters and their families—decided that their presently recognized obligation had no standing on this account, since the result would be that as things now stand, no one at all would take the responsibility. Again, if everyone recognized an obligation to share in duties pertaining to national defense, it would be morally acceptable to require this legally; but it would hardly be morally acceptable to do so if there are pacifists who on moral grounds are ready to die rather than bear arms. And similarly for other matters about which there are existing and pronounced moral convictions.

It seems clear that some modification must be made if our rule-utilitarian proposal is to have implications consistent with the moral convictions of thoughtful people. Unfortunately it is not clear just what the modification should be. The one I am inclined to adopt is as follows. First, we must drop that part of our conception which assumes that people in our hypothetical societies are of ordinary conscientiousness. We want to allow for the existence of both saints and sinners and to have a moral code to cope with them. In order to do this, we had better move closer to Urmson's original suggestion. We had better drop the notion of "adoption" and replace it by his term "recognition," meaning by "recognition by all" simply "belief by all that the rules formulate moral requirements." Second, we must avoid the conception of the acceptance of all the rules of a given moral code by *everybody* and replace it by something short of this, something which does not rule out the problems created by actual convictions about morals. Doing so means a rather uneasy compromise, because we cannot sacrifice the central feature of the rule-utilitarian view, which is that the rightness of an act is to be tested by whether it conforms with rules the (somehow) general acceptance of which would maximize utility. The compromise I propose is this: that the test whether an act is right is whether it is compatible with that set of rules which, were it to replace the moral commitments of members of the *actual society* at the time, *except where there are already fairly decided moral convictions,* would maximize utility.

The modified theory, then, is this: "An act is right if and only if it conforms with that learnable set of rules, the recognition of which as morally binding, roughly at the time of the act, by all actual people insofar as these rules are not incompatible with existing fairly decided moral commitments, would maximize intrinsic value." [7]

The modification has the effect that whether an act is right depends to some extent on such things as (1) how large a proportion of the actual population is conscientious and (2) what are the existing fairly decided moral beliefs at the time. This result is not obviously a mistake.

6. SECOND PROBLEM: CONFLICTS OF RULES

The objection is sure to be raised against any rule-utilitarian theory of the general sort we are considering that the whole conception is radically misconceived. For the theory proposes that what makes an act right is its conformity to the set of rules, recognition of which would maximize utility; and it is proposed that if we are in serious doubt whether an action would be right, we should ask ourselves whether it would conform with a utility-maximizing set of rules.

---

[7] This formulation is rather similar in effect to one suggested to me by Wilfrid Sellars. (I have no idea whether he now inclines toward it, or whether he ever did lean toward it strongly.) This is: "An act is right if and only if it conforms with that set of rules the *teaching of which* to the society of the agent, at the time of the action, would maximize welfare." This formulation is simpler, but it has its own problems. Teaching to which and how many individuals? By whom? With what skill and means? We should remember that it may be unwise to teach children the rules that are best for adults and that it may sometimes be desirable to teach ideals which are more extreme than we want people actually to live by, *e.g.,* those of the Sermon on the Mount.

Now, the objection will run, the very conception of such a set of rules evaporates, or else appears to involve contradictions, when we try to get it in sharp focus. The very idea of a set of rules simple enough to be learned and different from act-utilitarianism, and at the same time sufficiently comprehensive and precise to yield directions for conduct in every situation which may arise, is an impossible dream.

The reason is that moral problems are often quite complex. There are pros and cons—obligations and counterobligations— which have to be weighed delicately. For instance, a promise that has been made to do something is normally a point in favor of saying that doing it is obligatory; but just how much force the promise will have depends on various circumstances, such as when it was made, how solemnly it was made, whether it was fully understood by both parties, and so forth. The force of these circumstances cannot be stated and weighed by any set of rules. There is a moral to be drawn, it may be said, from W. D. Ross's theory of *prima facie* obligations: Ross could provide no general direction for what to do when *prima facie* obligations conflict; he had to leave the resolution of such conflicts to conscience or intuition. So, in general, no code simple enough to be written down and learned (and different from act-utilitarianism) can prescribe what is right in complex cases.

The difficulty is obviously a serious one. If the very concept of a complete code, the recognition of which would maximize utility, cannot be explained in detail, then the proposal that the rightness of every action is fixed by its conformity with the provisions of such a code must be abandoned.

What must be done to meet this charge? Of course, it cannot be demanded that we actually produce the ideal moral code for our society, or even a complete code of which the correct code might be supposed to be a variation. What can be fairly demanded is that we describe classes of rules or elements which may be expected in the ideal code, and that we make clear, in the course of this description, that the rules constituting the classes are simple enough to be learned, and that a person who had learned the rules of the several classes would be in a position to give an answer to all moral questions—or at least as definite an answer as can reasonably be expected. We may suppose that, if the theory is to be plausible, these classes of rules will be familiar—that they will be rules which thoughtful people do use in deciding moral issues. Let us see what can be said.

It is clear that a complete moral code must contain rules or principles of more than one level. The lowest level will consist of rules devised to cover familiar recurrent situations, presumably rather like those proposed by Ross in his formulation of *prima facie* obligations. Thus, it will contain rules like "Do not injure conscious beings," "Do what you have promised to do," and so forth. On reflection, we can see that such rules must be qualified in two ways. First, each of them must conclude with an exceptive clause something like "except as otherwise provided in this code." But second, they must be more complex than our samples; as Ross well knew, such simple rules do not state accurately what we think are our *prima facie* obligations—and presumably such rules are not the rules it would maximize welfare to have recognized as first-order rules. Consider for instance the rule I have suggested about promises. It is too simple, for we do not seriously believe that *all* promises have even a *prima facie* claim to be fulfilled; nor would it be a good thing for people to think they ought. For instance, we think there is no obligation at all to keep a promise made on the basis of deliberate misrepresentation by the promisee; and it is to the public interest that we should think as we do. Just as the law of contracts lists various types of contracts which it is against the public interest for the courts to enforce, so there are types of promises the fulfillment of which we do not think obligatory, and a moral requirement to fulfill them would be contrary to the public interest. The lowest-level group of rules, then, will include one about promise-keeping which will state explicitly which types of promises must be kept except when some more stringent obligation intervenes. And the same for the other basic moral rules.

I do not know if anyone would contend that it would be impossible to write down an exact statement formulating our total *prima facie* obligations—the kinds of considerations which to some extent make a moral claim on agents. I do not know if anyone would say that in principle we cannot state exactly the list of *prima facie* obligations it would maximize utility for everyone to feel. Whether or not anyone does say that a list of exact *prima facie* obligations cannot be stated, I know of no solid argument which can be put forward to show that this is the case. I do not believe a satisfactory list *has* been provided (Ross's statement being quite abbreviated), but I know of no sound reason for thinking that it cannot be. It would not, I think, be an impossible inquiry to determine what is the total set of distinct fundamental *prima facie* obligations people in fact do recognize in their moral thinking.

A set of first-level rules, however, is not enough. For moral perplexities arise most often where there are conflicts of *prima facie* obligations, where there would be conflicts of the first-level moral rules. If the rule-utilitarian theory is to work, it must provide for the resolution of such perplexities. How can this be done?

The problem can be partially met by supposing that a complete moral code will contain second-level rules specifically prescribing for conflicts of the basic rules. One second-level rule might be: "Do not injure anyone solely in order to produce something good, unless the good achieved be substantially greater than the injury." In fact we already learn and believe rules roughly of this kind. For instance, Ross suggested in *The Right and the Good* that we think there is normally a stronger obligation to avoid injury to others than to do good or to keep one's promises. A moral code can contain some such second-order rules without intolerable complexity.

But such rules will hardly be numerous enough to solve all the problems. And the rule we stated was not precise: it used the vague phrase "substantially greater," which is clear enough, in context, to decide for many situations, but it is by no means precise enough to legislate for all. I think, therefore, that if the very conception of a set of rules simple enough to be learned and adequate to adjudicate all possible cases is to be intelligible, it must be possible to formulate a consistent and plausible "remainder-rule," that is, a top-level rule giving adequate directions for all cases for which the lower-level rules do not prescribe definitely enough or for which their prescriptions are conflicting. We are not here called upon to identify the correct remainder-rule—although we know that the rule-utilitarian theory is that the correct one is the one the recognition of which (*etc.*) would do most good. What we are called upon to do is to sketch out what such a rule might well be like.

It is worthwhile to mention two possibilities for a remainder-rule.[8] First, such a rule might specify that all cases not legislated for by other clauses in the code be decided simply on the basis of comparative utility of consequences. For such cases, then, the remainder-rule would prescribe exactly what the act-utilitarian principle prescribes. Second (and I think this possibility the more interesting), the remainder-rule might be: "One is obligated to perform an action if and only if a person who knew the relevant facts and had them vividly in mind, had been carefully taught the other rules of this code, and was uninfluenced by interests beyond those arising from learning the code, would feel obligated to perform that action." Such a rule could decide cases not legislated for by the remainder of the code only if the explicit rules were taught so as to be connected with different degrees of *felt obligation*. In some cases such an association could be established by the very content of the rule, for instance, in the case of a rule stating that there is an obligation not to injure others, and that the obligation increases in strength with the amount of injury involved. Another example is that of second-level rules about the priorities of first-level rules. In other cases the association might be fixed simply by the relative insistence or firmness of the teachers, with respect to the rule in question. As a result of the rules being taught in this way, conscientious people would have established in them hesitations, of different degrees of strength, to do certain sorts of things—in other words, a sense of obligation to do or avoid certain things, the sense having different force for different things. Therefore, when persons so trained were faced with a situation in which lower-order rules gave conflicting directions (and where no higher-order rule assigned an explicit priority), they would hesitate to resolve the problem in various ways because of the built-in sense of obligation. Now, the proposed remainder-rule would in effect be a somewhat qualified prescription to take whatever course of action would leave morally well-trained people least dissatisfied. (I imagine that some-

[8] It will probably be clear why the remainder-rule cannot simply be the rule-utilitarian principle itself. For the rule-utilitarian principle states that an act is right if and only if it conforms with the rules of a certain kind of code. If one of the rules of the code were the rule-utilitarian principle, it would contain reference to a code which presumably would itself contain again the rule-utilitarian principle, and so on *ad infinitum*.

thing like this is what Ross had in mind when he said that in complex situations one must rely on one's intuition.) The rule-utilitarian proposal is, of course, that the correct degree of felt obligation to be associated with a rule is, like the order of priorities expressed in the second-level rules, fixed by the relative utilities of the various possible arrangements—partly the utilities of the adjudications of complex cases by the remainder-rule.

It is after all possible, then, for a moral code different from act-utilitarianism to be simple enough to be learned and still able to decide for all problems which may arise.

7. THIRD PROBLEM: RELATIVITY TO THE AGENT'S SOCIETY

One final complication may be needed in the rule-utilitarian proposal. In place of saying that the rightness of an act is fixed by conformity with the prescriptions of the moral code, the recognition of which as morally binding by people (*etc.*) *everywhere* would maximize intrinsic good, we might say that the rightness of an act is fixed by conformity with the prescriptions of that moral code, the recognition of which as morally binding by people *in the agent's society* would maximize intrinsic good. This kind of complication should be avoided if possible, because it is difficult to assign a definite meaning to the phrase "in the agent's society." We should notice, incidentally, that it is *not* suggested that the test be the maximizing of intrinsic good only in the agent's society; such a thesis would promise quite dubious consequences.

A modification of this sort would admit a kind of relativism into ethics. For, while it is consistent with the rule-utilitarian principle itself being correct for everyone, it has the consequence that an act might be right in one society which would be wrong in another society. For instance, it might be a moral obligation for a man to support his elderly father in one society, but not his obligation in another society. Most philosophers, however, would probably view this kind of relativism as innocuous, since such differences in obligation could occur only when conditions in the two societies were different in such a way that recognition of one rule by one society would have best consequences, and recognition of a different rule by another society would also have best consequences.

But is there any reason for adopting this complicating feature? Why not say that, if a moral code is valid for anybody it is valid for everybody? Surely, it will be said, *some* moral rules are universally valid—perhaps, for instance, a rule forbidding a person from causing another pain merely in order to give himself pleasure. And if so, perhaps we can go on, with Ross, to say that the fundamental principles of obligation are universally true, although their application in special circumstances may give rise to an *appearance* of society-bound rules. For instance, Ross would say that "Keep your promises" is universally a true and important first-level rule. But in some places a thing is promised with certain mutually understood but not explicitly stated conditions, while in other places the implicit conditions are different. As a result, the conduct required, in view of the explicit promise, by the universally valid principle is different in different societies. Or again, "Thou shalt not steal" or "Thou shalt not commit adultery" might be construed as universally valid injunctions, the first being not to take property which, according to the institutions of the society, is recognized as belonging to another, and the second, not to have sexual relations with any person if either party is, according to the custom of the society, the marriage partner of another. All fundamental moral principles, then, may be thought to have intersocietal validity; only the specific conduct enjoined or prohibited may vary from one society to another because of local conditions.

This view, however, faces serious difficulties. In order to bring these into focus, let us consider an example: the obligations of a father to his children. In the United States, I believe, it is thought that a father should see to it—within the limits of his financial capacities—that his children receive a good education, enjoy physical and mental health, and have some security against unforeseeable catastrophes. Contrast this with a society, like that of the Hopi, in which responsibility for children falls primarily on a household, "household" being defined primarily by blood-ties with the mother. In this situation, responsibility for children is primarily a problem for the mother and her blood relatives. (The factual accuracy of these assertions is not, I believe, a material consideration.) In the United States, the father is generally charged with responsibility for bringing the welfare, or prospects of welfare, of his children up to a certain rough minimum; in the Hopi society this responsibility falls roughly on other persons, although the father may share in it as far as affection dictates. Correspondingly, in the United States grown children have responsibility for their father, whereas among the Hopi the responsibility for the father belongs elsewhere—not on a man's own children but on the household of the father, the one to which he belongs through blood-ties with his mother and siblings.

I take it nobody is going to argue that fathers in the United States do not have the obligations they are generally thought to have, or that Hopi fathers do have obligations which are generally thought to fall elsewhere. (There may be some exceptions to this.) Therefore, if there is to be a *universal* moral rule locating obligations for the welfare of children, it will be one which roughly places it, at least for the present, where it is recognized to be in these societies. What kind of rule might this be? It is hard to say. Very possibly there is uniformity of assignment of such responsibilities in societies with a certain kind of social structure, and hence one could conceivably state a general rule prescribing that fathers do certain things in societies of a specified sociological description. It is doubtful, however, whether such a rule is simple enough to be learned. Moreover, social structures may be too much organic wholes to permit even such generalizations; if so, in respect of some kinds of conduct there can be no general, intersocietally valid moral rule at all.

There is another way of putting much the same point. Instead of asking whether we can frame a general rule which will have implications for particular societies coincident with what we should want to say are the actual locations of responsibilities in these societies, we might ask whether any universal rules can be framed, recognition of which as morally binding would have consequences comparably as good as local rules, devised on the basis of examination of individual institutional structures as a whole. Is the universality of moral rules to be so sacrosanct that we shall not recognize a moral rule as binding on a given society unless it can be viewed as a special case of some universally valid rule? A person who wishes to make utility the test of moral rules will, I think, wish to make the utility of local rules his test.

It may be supposed that the example of family obligations is untypically complex. But to do so would be a mistake. The responsibilities of physicians and teachers—or professional men in general —to the individuals whom they serve pose similar difficulties. So do the ethics of borrowing and the charging of interest. It is possible that the broad outlines of prohibited and required behavior will be rather similar in all societies. But when we come to the fine points—the exceptions, the qualifications, the priorities—we are in for difficulties if we must defend the view that statable universal rules are the best ones for everybody to feel bound by, or that they conform to serious opinions about the location of obligations in various types of society. This, I think, has been the conclusion of various "self-realizationist" philosophers like A. MacBeath and C. A. Campbell.

Let us then consider (without necessarily insisting that it be adopted) the view that the rightness of an act is fixed by conformity with the prescriptions of that moral code, the recognition of which as morally binding by people (*etc.*) *in the agent's society* would maximize intrinsic good. Can we propose a meaning of "in the agent's society" sufficiently definite that we can say the proposal is at least a clear one?

How shall we identify "the society" of the agent? This question could have been answered fairly simply in much earlier times when all societies were rather clearly demarcated atomic units, although when we remember the relationships of the *kula* reported by Malinowski, we can see that matters were not always so simple even among primitive peoples. The question is difficult in a modern civilization. What is a Columbia University professor who lives in the suburbs to count as his "society"? The faculty club? His suburb? New York City? The state of New York? Any choice seems a bit arbitrary. Or suppose Khrushchev makes a promise to Eisenhower. What society should we bear in mind as the one the utility of a set of rules in which sets the standard of right and wrong?

Very tentatively, I am inclined to suggest that we understand the "society of an agent" in the following way. An individual, I suggest, may live in several "moral worlds," and the rules for these several moral worlds may be different. For one thing, he is a member of a succession of local groups, each one more inclusive than the last: the local community, the metropolitan area, and so forth. Now a good part of one's life is lived as a resident, a neighbor, a citizen. Insofar as moral problems arise as part of one's life in this capacity, the problem is to be settled by reference to the rules best for the geographical community. How wide a geographical community should we pick? The best answer seems to be: the largest area over which common rules can be adopted without loss of utility. If it were costly in utility to apply to a borough the rules which were the best for the metropolitan area, then we had better consider our case in the light of rules useful for the smaller group. But a person has other roles besides that of citizen and neighbor. One may be a member of groups which transcend the local community—perhaps nation-wide associations, class, or caste. Most important, perhaps, are transactions resulting from the institutional involvement of the participants; for example, business transactions involving corporations or unions, or the affairs of the church, or educational affairs, or the activities of the press or radio. In these cases a segment of the life-relations of the individuals involved consists in their interactions with others who have the same role or who participate in the same institution. In such cases, I suggest that the moral rules governing behavior should be the rules adoption of which by the relevant group (for example, the group participating in a given institution) would be best, as governing the transactions of that group. It may be, of course, that we do not need some of these complications, that there is no need to distinguish the rules for businessmen in dealing with each other or with a union from the ones properly followed in one's relations with wife and neighbor.[9]

8. CONCLUDING REMARKS

The principle with which we end is this: "An act is right if and only if it conforms with that learnable set of rules the recognition

[9] The above discussion shows that the theory that what is right is behavior conforming with the *accepted* rules of the agent's society has complications which have not been adequately discussed.

of which as morally binding—roughly at the time of the act—by everyone in the society of the agent, except for the retention by individuals of already formed and decided moral convictions, would maximize intrinsic value." [10]

I wish to make three final comments on this principle.

First, one may ask whether a set of moral rules which would maximize intrinsic value in the way described would necessarily be a *just* set of rules. Surely, if the rules are not just, conformity with them will by no means guarantee that an action is right. A further inquiry must be made about whether additional requirements are needed to assure that moral rules are just. It may be that, as I have suggested elsewhere, none is called for if equality of some sort is an intrinsic good.

Second, if the proposed principle is correct, we can give at least a partial answer to a person who asks *why* he ought to perform actions he is obligated to perform, if they conflict with his self-interest. Perhaps a person who asks such a question is merely confused, and his query not worth our attention. But we can say to him that one reason for meeting his obligation is that by doing so he plays the game of living according to the rules which will maximize welfare. And this will be, at least partially, a satisfying answer to a man who is activated by love or sympathy or respect directed at other sentient beings generally.

Finally, some reflections on the employment of the principle. It is, perhaps, obvious that it is not necessary to advocate that everyone always bear the rule-utilitarian principle in mind in deciding what he ought to do. Not that it would be harmful—beyond the waste of time—to do so; for it is obvious that the clear moral obligations are prescribed by the principle. For example, only an instant's thought is required to see that it is socially useful to recognize the rule that solemn promises should be kept—doubtless with some qualifications. The rule's employment is important, however, in analyzing more difficult cases, in making clear whether a given moral rule should be qualified in a certain way. Of course, it would be foolish to suggest that application of the principle is an easy road to the resolution of moral problems. It may very often be that

---

[10] As the principle now stands, a given individual might have to learn several codes, corresponding to his several roles in society.

after most careful reflection along the lines suggested, the most that can be said is that a given action is probably the one which the principle requires. If so, if we accept the principle, we can go on to say that this action is probably the right one.

Bibliographical Essay

This bibliography is intended as an introduction to, rather than a comprehensive survey of, the literature on the problems with which we have been concerned. The reader who wants further bibliographical information should consult the bibliographies of the books mentioned below.

There are several good texts on ethics that provide useful introductions to the problems discussed in this book, as well as to other problems in ethics. These include: R. BRANDT's *Ethical Theory* (Englewood Cliffs, N.J.: Prentice-Hall, Inc., 1959), W. FRANKENNA's *Ethics* (Englewood Cliffs, N.J.: Prentice-Hall, Inc., 1966), R. GARNER and B. ROSEN's *Moral Philosophy* (New York: The Macmillan Company, 1967), and J. HOSPER's *Human Conduct* (New York: Harcourt, Brace & World, Inc., 1961). In connection with these books, the student might profitably consult some of the selections in the following anthologies: R. BRANDT's *Value and Obligation* (New York: Harcourt, Brace & World, Inc., 1961), G. DWORKIN and J. THOMSON's *Ethics* (Harper & Row, Publishers, 1968), J. MARGOLIS's *Contemporary Ethical Theory* (Random House, Inc., 1966), A. I. MELDEN's *Ethical Theories* (Englewood Cliffs, N.J.: Prentice-Hall, Inc., 1950), W. SELLARS and J. HOSPER's *Readings in Ethical Theory* (New York: Appleton-Century-Crofts, 1952), and P. TAYLOR's *The Moral Judgement* (Englewood Cliffs, N.J.: Prentice-Hall, Inc., 1963).

Kant's major works in moral philosophy are *Foundations of the*

Metaphysics of Morals, Critique of Practical Reason, Metaphysical Elements of Justice, and *Metaphysical Principles of Virtue.* All of these books are readily available in good translations in Library of Liberal Arts paper editions. Some of the most helpful commentaries on Kant's ethical views are L. W. BECK's *A Commentary on Kant's Critique of Practical Reason* (Chicago: University of Chicago Press, 1960), M. J. GREGOR's *Laws of Freedom* (New York: Barnes & Noble, Inc., 1963), and H. J. PATON's *The Categorical Imperative* (Chicago: University of Chicago Press, 1948). Several important articles on Kant's ethical views are collected in R. P. WOLFF's *Kant* (Garden City, N.Y.: Doubleday-Anchor Books, 1967). The reader might also consult the following recent articles that seem quite helpful: R. HALL's "Kant and Ethical Formalism" *Kant Studien* (1960–61), H. J. PATON's "An Alleged Right to Lie: A Problem in Kantian Ethics" *Kant Studien* (1953–54), and M. SINGER's "The Categorical Imperative" *Philosophical Review* (1954).

The classical statements of the act-utilitarian position are J. BENTHAM's *An Introduction to the Principles of Morals and Legislation* (New York: Hafner Publishing Co., Inc., 1948), J. S. MILL's *Utilitarianism* (Library of Liberal Arts, 1957), G. E. MOORE's *Ethics* (Home University Library, 1912), and H. SIDGWICK's *The Methods of Ethics* (New York: The Macmillan Company, 1962). It should be noted that J. O. URMSON, in "The Interpretation of the Moral Philosophy of J. S. Mill" *Philosophical Quarterly* (1953), has argued that Mill was really a rule-utilitarian. This interpretation is challenged by J. D. MABBOT in "Interpretations of Mill's Utilitarianism" *Philosophical Quarterly* (1956). An important recent defence of the act-utilitarian position is J. J. C. SMART's *An Outline of a System of Utilitarian Ethics* (Melbourne University Press, 1961).

Ross developed his views in his two books, *The Right and the Good* (Oxford: The Clarendon Press, 1930) and *Foundations of Ethics* (Oxford: The Clarendon Press, 1939). His position is criticized in W. PICKARD-CAMBRIDGE's "Two Problems about Duty" *Mind* (1932).

Some of the influential statements of rule-utilitarianism are found in R. F. HARROD's "Utilitarianism Revisited" *Mind* (1936), J. D. MABBOT's "Moral Rules" *Proceedings of the British Academy*

(1953), J. RAWLS's "Two Concepts of Rules" *Philosophical Review* (1955), and S. TOULMIN's *An Examination of the Place of Reason in Ethics* (Cambridge University Press, 1950). The position is criticized in A. DUNCAN JONES's "Utilitarianism and Rules" *Philosophical Quarterly* (1957), H. G. McCLOSKEY's "An Examination of Restricted Utilitarianism" *Philosophical Review* (1957), and J. MARGOLIS's "Rule Utilitarianism" *Australasian Journal of Philosophy* (1965). Brandt's type of criticism is developed at much greater length in D. LYONS's *Forms and Limits of Utilitarianism* (Clarendon Press: 1965) and criticized in B. A. BRODY's "The Equivalence of Act and Rule Utilitarianism" *Philosophical Studies* (1967).